The Real Truth About Germany: Facts About The War

Douglas Brooke Wheelton Sladen

The Real
"Truth About Germany"

Facts About the War

By

Douglas Sladen

An Analysis and a Refutation from the English Point of View,
of the Pamphlet "The Truth About Germany,"
Issued under the Authority of a Committee
of Representative German Citizens

With an Appendix

Great Britain and the War

By

A. Maurice Low, M.A.

G. P. Putnam's Sons
New York and London
The Knickerbocker Press
1914

The Knickerbocker Press, New York

PUBLISHERS' NOTE

THE following volume contains a reprint of the text of a pamphlet recently issued in Germany (in English) under the authority of a committee of representative citizens. It carries the names of the following Editors: Paul Dehn, Dr. Drechsler, Matthias Erzberger, Dr. Francke, B. Huldermann, Dr. Jäckh, D. Naumann, Graf von Oppersdorff, Graf zu Reventlow, Dr. Paul Rohrbach, Dr. Schacht.

It may fairly be described as the official German justification of the war.

This pamphlet, while not formally published, is being distributed throughout the United States, but pains have apparently been taken to prevent copies finding their way into Great Britain. It is on this ground that the monograph is referred to by the English commentator as the "Secret White Paper." The analysis, made by a well-known English writer of the statements, facts, and conclusions presented by the German Committee, should prove of interest to American as well as to English readers. In this form of statement and answer, the volume constitutes an important contribution for the use of the future historian.

iii

The statements of the German writer, or writers, are printed in Roman type, while the text in heavy face represents the comments and replies of Mr. Sladen.

The publishers have thought it desirable to include in the volume, for the purpose of giving to the presentation of the case against Germany a full measure of completeness, a statement from the well-known writer Mr. A. Maurice Low, who discusses without heat, but with the authority of a scholarly publicist, the evidence and the documents on the causation of the war and the relative responsibilities of England and of Germany.

NEW YORK,
October 5, 1914.

PREFACE

WITH the apparent purpose of misleading the American public as to the real factors which brought about the war, a monograph has been brought into print in Germany under the supervision of a Committee of Representative Germans, including Prince von Bülow, the German Imperial Chancellor from 1900 to 1909, entitled *Truth About Germany. Facts About the War.*

The book carries no title-page, or publishing imprint or place of issue, and care has been taken to prevent it from reaching England. The edition has, however, been distributed widely in America, and copies were handed to certain American visitors (apparently those whom the German authorities thought could be trusted) as they left Germany.

Realizing the harm that could be caused by a series of erroneous and misleading statements, I have arranged with Messrs. Hutchinson, in London, and with G. P. Putnam's Sons, in New York, to publish an edition of a book which should contain the exact text of the *Truth About Germany*, with the misstatements corrected paragraph by paragraph. The reader will note that many of these refutations are not in my words, but are extracts from the utterances, speeches, and letters of public men.   A number of them are taken from White Books and from Official Reports.

The present volume is the only form in which *Truth About Germany* can at this time be procured in Great Britain.   Its introduction here was apparently prohibited by the German authorities, who realized how promptly the misstatements contained in the volume would be refuted in the English press.   Every word of the original book will be found faithfully reprinted in this volume, and the text of the statements as originally given is followed by the analyses and refutations.

As one example of the trustworthiness of the statements in *Truth About Germany*, I need at this point quote but one sentence:

"The German troops with their iron discipline will respect the personal property and liberty of the individual in Belgium as they did in France in 1870."

As evidence of the trustworthiness of this promise, I need only refer to the record of German operations in Louvain, Malines, Dinant, Aerschot, and Termonde.   These towns were destroyed not through the unavoidable waste of battle, but under official orders.   There may also well be question as to whether the guaranty will provide insurance for the destruction of the Cathedral of Rheims.

DOUGLAS SLADEN.

LONDON,
September 23, 1914.

vii

COUNT VON SCHWERIN LÖWITZ, President of the House of
Deputies.

WILHELM VON SIEMENS, Berlin.

FREDERICK, PRINCE ZU SOLMS-BARUTH.

MAX WARBURG, Hamburg.

SIEGFRIED WAGNER, Bayreuth.

VON WILAMOWITZ-MOELLENDORFF, Berlin.

PROF. DR. WUNDY, Leipzig.

FRAU GOLDBERGER (wife of Privy Councillor of Commerce G.),
Berlin.

PRINCESS HENCKEL VON DONNERSMARCK.

THE DUCHESS OF RATIBOR.

THE BARONESS SPECK VON STERNBURG.

FRAU VON TROTT ZU SOLZ (wife of v. Trott z. Solz, Minister of
State).

BOARD OF EDITORS

PAUL DEHN, Author, Berlin.

DR. DRECHSLER, Director of the American Institute, Berlin.

MATTHIAS ERZBERGER, Member of the Reichstag, Berlin.

PROF. DR. FRANCKE, Berlin.

B. HULDERMANN, Director of the Hamburg-American Steamship
Company, Berlin.

DR. ERNST JÄCKH, Berlin.

D. NAUMANN, Member of the Reichstag, Berlin.

COUNT VON OPPERSDORFF, Member of the Prussian Upper House
and Member of the Reichstag, Berlin.

COUNT ZU REVENTLOW, Author, Charlottenburg.

DR. PAUL ROHRBACH, Dozent of the High School of Commerce,
Berlin.

DR. SCHACHT, Director of the Bank of Dresden, Berlin.

CONTENTS

INTRODUCTION

FROM HEINE TO VON BERNHARDI

THE PROPHECY OF HEINE

"Christianity—and this is its highest merit—
has in some degree softened, but it could not
destroy, that brutal German joy of battle. When
once the taming talisman, the Cross, breaks in
two, the savagery of the old fighters, the senseless
Berserker fury of which the northern poets sing
and say so much, will gush up anew. That talisman is decayed, and the day will come when it
will piteously collapse. Then the old stone gods
will rise from the silent ruins, and rub the dust
of a thousand years from their eyes. Thor, with
his giant's hammer, will at last spring up, and
shatter to bits the Gothic cathedrals."—*Quoted in
a letter to "The Times," September 21st, 1914.*

WHAT VON BERNHARDI SAYS

"We may expect from the Government that it
will prosecute the military and political preparations for war with the energy which the situation
demands, in clear knowledge of the dangers
threatening us, but also in correct appreciation of
our national needs and of the warlike strength of
our people, and that it will not let any conventional
scruples distract it from this object."

"Conditions may arise which are more powerful than the most honorable intentions."

"Our people must learn to see that *the maintenance of peace never can be or may be the goal of a policy.*"

"The inevitableness, the idealism, and the blessing of war, as an indispensable and stimulating law of development, must be repeatedly emphasized."

"The lessons of history thus confirm the view that wars which have been deliberately provoked by far-seeing statesmen have had the happiest results."

"Such decision is rendered more easy by the consideration that the prospects of success are always the greatest when the moment for declaring war can be settled to suit the political and military situation."

"Reflection thus shows not only that war is an unqualified necessity, but that it is justifiable from every point of view."

"If we sum up our arguments, we shall see that, from the most opposite aspects, the efforts directed towards the abolition of war must not only be termed foolish, but absolutely immoral, and must be stigmatized as unworthy of the human race."

These quotations are not continuous, but specimens of what may be found on almost every page in von Bernhardi's "Germany and the Next War." To them may be added, since, the destruction of Louvain, Malines, Termonde, Dinant, and Rheims Cathedral:

"I must try to prove that war is not merely a necessary element in the life of nations, but an indispensable factor of culture, in which a true civilized nation finds the highest expression of strength and vitality."—VON BERNHARDI.

"My heart bleeds for Louvain."—THE KAISER.

FOREWORD TO CHAPTER I

The Times in a dispatch from its correspondent in New York on August 13th, 1914, says:

"The *Outlook* (New York) to-day publishes a careful symposium setting forth the case for every nation engaged in the war. It follows this with a leading article, entitled 'The War against Popular Rights,' in which it says:

"'History will hold the German Emperor responsible for the war in Europe. Austria would never have made her indefensible attack on Servia if she had not been assured beforehand of the support of Germany. The German Emperor's consent to co-operate with England in mediation could have put a stop to Austria's advance. To doubt that Germany and Austria have been in practical alliance in this act of brigandage—for it deserves no other name—is to shut one's eyes to all the signs. The inevitable consequences of the Austro-German alliance, if it is successful, it required no prophet to see. It would reduce the Balkan States to the state of provinces of Germany and Austria. It would make Belgium and Holland Germanic provinces. It would create a Germanic Empire which would extend from the North Sea to the Mediterranean. It would bring all Europe under the domination of this Germanic Empire, and would reduce Italy, Spain, Portugal, France, and England to subordinate positions, if it did not make them dependencies. It would banish from Eastern Europe the democratic movement in which France and England are the leaders. It would discourage the hopes of the democracy in Spain, Italy, and Russia, and would enthrone autocracy from the Atlantic coast to Siberia, from the North Sea to the Mediterranean.

"'Because the German Emperor combines with remarkable ability for organization this mediæval ambition to dominate all Europe, he is the greatest personal peril of the century to popular liberty and human development. . . .'"

The Real Truth About Germany*

CHAPTER I

LISTEN, ALL YE PEOPLE!

TRY to realize, everyone of you, what we are
going through! Only a few weeks ago all
of us were peacefully following our several voca-
tions. The peasant was gathering in this summer's
peaceful crop, the factory hand was working with
accustomed vigor. Not one human being amongst
us dreamed of war.

**"Not one human being amongst us dreamed
of war." This sentence excludes a great many
otherwise worthy persons from the category of
human beings, for mobilization notices had gone
out to Germans in South America in time to get
them home for the war—a matter of two months,
at least. And one wonders what the people who
were making the big siege-guns were thinking of.**

We are a nation that wishes to lead a quiet
and industrial life. This need hardly be stated

*The text of the German statement is printed in the roman
type; and that of the British comment in the heavy face.

3

to you Americans. You, of all others, know the
temper of the German who lives within your gates.
Our love of peace is so strong that it is not regarded by us in the light of a virtue; we simply
know it to be an inborn and integral portion of
ourselves. Since the foundation of the German
Empire in the year 1871, we, living in the center
of Europe, have given an example of tranquillity
and peace, never once seeking to profit by any
momentary difficulties of our neighbors.

> " Never once seeking to profit by any momen-
> tary difficulties of our neighbors." On pain of
> war Germany forced France to dismiss M. Del-
> cassé from office at the time of the first Morocco
> incident; on pain of war, she forced Russia
> (whom she had egged on into her disastrous Man-
> churia Expedition with the express purpose of
> weakening her) to acquiesce in Austria's piratical
> seizure of Bosnia and the Herzegovina in 1908.
> She seized a port in Morocco with the object of
> applying similar pressure to France in the Agadir
> incident three years ago, but compromised when
> she found that war with France meant war also
> with Great Britain, whom she had treated as a
> negligible quantity; and caused the present war by
> trying to humiliate Russia as she had humiliated
> her in 1909. And to crown all one may mention
> the Emperor's telegram to President Kruger at
> the time of the Jameson Raid, and his proposal to
> France and Russia that they should join him in
> annihilating England when she was paralyzed by
> the Boer War.

Our commercial extension, our financial rise in the world, is far removed from any love of adventure, it is the fruit of painstaking and plodding labor.

> " Our commercial extension is far removed from any love of adventure." The seizure of Kiao-Chau, the German territory in China which Japan is now besieging, is a sufficient example to the contrary.

We are not credited with this temper, because we are insufficiently known. Our situation and **our way of thinking** is not easily grasped.

Everyone is aware that we have produced great philosophers and poets, **we have preached the gospel of humanity** with impassioned zeal. America fully appreciates Goethe and Kant, looks upon them as corner-stones of elevated culture. Do you really believe that we have changed our natures, that our souls can be satisfied with military drill and servile obedience? We are soldiers, because we have to be soldiers, because otherwise Germany and **German civilization** would be swept away from the face of the earth. It has cost us long and weary struggles to attain our independence, and we know full well that in order to preserve it we must not content ourselves with building schools and factories, we must look to our garrisons and forts. We and all our soldiers have remained, however, the same lovers of music and lovers of exalted thought. We have retained our old devotion to all peaceable sciences and arts: as all the world knows, we work in the foremost rank of those who strive to advance the exchange of commodities, who further useful, technical knowledge.

> **Other nations have not seen the phases of the German character alluded to in the above paragraph. But they will readily admit the sacrifices of universal service and heavy taxation to which the Germans so cheerfully submit, so as to be able to fight their Eastern and Western neighbors at the same time, and that Germany has maintained the most perfect military organization known in history without losing ground in Music or Learning, Art or Science.**

But we have been forced to become a nation of soldiers, in order to be free. And we are bound to follow our Kaiser, because he symbolizes and represents the unity of our nation. To-day, knowing no distinction of party, no difference of opinion, we rally round him, willing to shed the last drop of our blood. For though it takes a great deal to rouse us Germans, when once aroused our feelings run deep and strong. Everyone is filled with this passion, with the soldier's ardor. But when the waters of the deluge shall have subsided, gladly will we return to the plow, and to the anvil.

> **All foreigners will agree that it is because the Germans felt themselves bound to follow their**

Kaiser blindly that the present war has ensued.
But it is difficult for them to take the view that it
needs much to rouse German arrogance, which
has hung over the head of Europe like the sword
of Damocles for nearly half a century.

It deeply distresses us to see two highly-civilized
nations, England and France, joining the onslaught
of autocratic Russia. That this could happen,
will remain one of the anomalies of history. It
is not our fault: we firmly believed in the desira-
bility of the great nations working together, we
peaceably came to terms with France and England
in sundry difficult African questions. There was
no cause for war between Western Europe and us,
no reason why Western Europe should feel itself
constrained to further the power of the Czar.

> That " highly-civilized " England and France
> find themselves allied in this war to " autocra-
> tic " Russia is no anomaly, because Germany has
> chosen to maintain an army which upset the
> balance of Europe without the army of Russia in
> the other scale. As to the difficult African ques-
> tions in which Germany peaceably came to terms
> with France and England, see page 115. Since
> England and France relied on the Czar, they had
> to support him when he was threatened with war
> or humiliation by Germany.

The Czar, as an individual, is most certainly
not the instigator of the unspeakable horrors that
are now inundating Europe. But he bears before

God and posterity the responsibility of having allowed himself to be terrorized by an unscrupulous military clique.

The English and the Americans consider that the man who has to bear before God and posterity the responsibility of listening to an unscrupulous military clique is, not the Czar, but the Kaiser—if, indeed, he had that excuse, and was not listening to the voice of the flatterers of his entourage even more than to the voice of his military advisers.

Ever since the weight of the crown has pressed upon him he has been the tool of others. He did not desire the brutalities in Finland, he did not approve of the iniquities of the Jewish Pogroms, but his hand was too weak to stop the fury of the reactionary party. Why would he not permit Austria to pacify her southern frontier? It was inconceivable that Austria should calmly see her heir-apparent murdered. How could she? All the nationalities under her rule realized the impossibility of tamely allowing Servia's only too evident and successful intrigues to be carried on under her very eyes. The Austrians could not allow their venerable and sorely-stricken monarch to be wounded and insulted any longer.

" Why would not the Czar permit Austria to pacify her southern frontier? " asks the pamphlet, very disingenuously. It is notorious that when Austria first sought satisfaction from Servia,

making the murder of the Archduke Francis
Ferdinand the occasion, Russia, in her anxiety
for the peace of Europe, brought considerable
pressure to bear on Servia, urging her to give
every reasonable satisfaction. Austria, however,
demanded almost impossible terms from Servia,
with an ultimatum of indecently short duration.
Nothing short of a humiliation so absolute that
the Balkan kingdoms would consider that Russia
had not the power to protect them would satisfy
Austria.

This reasonable and honorable sentiment on
the part of Austria has caused Russia to put itself
forward as the patron of Servia, as the enemy of
European thought and civilization.

Russia had the candor to admit that Servia had,
since her successes in two Balkan wars, been very
difficult in her attitude towards Austria. And
this she admitted not forgetting the provocation
Servia had received from Austria, not only by the
seizure of Bosnia and Herzegovina, but by being
denied access to the sea, after her sacrifices and
her heroic conduct in her two victorious wars.
She therefore tried to make Servia reasonable in
replying to the Austrian ultimatum. She was
even willing to let Austria chastise Servia, provided that after the chastisement had been inflicted she should be consulted as to the terms to
be imposed upon Servia. Less she could not do
without losing her position in Europe and especially in the Balkan peninsula. Undoubtedly the
Servian agitation in the South-Slav provinces of

Austria would have been extinguished as part of the pact.

We know now that Austria, if left to herself, would have been glad to accept Russia's offer, also that Austria advanced her claims at this moment in this peremptory way because Germany had decided either to fight Russia before her military strength was any further advanced, or to inflict another humiliation on her like that of 1909, which would make the Balkan Slavs abandon Russia.

Russia has an important mission to fill in its own country and in Asia.   It would do better in its own interest to leave the rest of the world in peace.   But the die is cast, and all nations must decide whether they wish to further us by senti- ments and by deeds, or the government of the Czar.   This is the real significance of this appal- ling struggle, all the rest is immaterial.   Russia's attitude alone has forced us to go to war with France, and with their great ally.

The die has been cast, and the principal nations of Europe and Asia have decided that the cause of civilization is to be served by supporting the Czar against the Kaiser. The gigantic armaments, the incessant war-scares, producing cataclysms on the Exchanges of Europe, the increasing fre- quency of ultimatums, make the establishment of a " pax Romana " a " sine qua non " for Europe. And this is only to be achieved by breaking up the military tyranny with which Germany has threatened it. This is not a war to save the skin of Servia or to further Pan-Slavism; it is a war against violence and military autocracy—a war to give the world rest.

" Russia's attitude alone " did force Germany into war with England and France because Russia defied the bully, and France would not forsake her; the actual occasion of England's declaration of war was Germany's violation of Belgian neutrality.

The German nation is serious and conscientious. Never would a German Government dare to contemplate a war for the sake of dynastic interest, or for the sake of glory. This would be against the entire bent of our character. Firmly believing in the justice of our cause, all parties—the Conservatives and the Clericals, the Liberals and the Socialists—have joined hands. All disputes are forgotten, one duty exists for all—the duty of defending our country and vanquishing the enemy.

Will not this calm, self-reliant, and unanimous readiness to sacrifice all, to die or win, appeal to other nations and force them to understand our real character and the situation in which we are placed?

The public opinion of Europe and America does not endorse the dictum of the pamphlet that " never would a German Government dare to contemplate a war for the sake of dynastic interest or for the sake of glory. " For surely the latter includes the reason for which this war is being waged. Germany, as von Bernhardi has pointed out again and again, has aimed at the hegemony of Europe developing into the hegemony of the world. The crushing of France, the absorption of Belgium, Holland, and Denmark, the stripping England of her navy, her colonies, and her wealth, were all steps in this peaceful aim. Then the United States were to be defied for the possession of South America. Russia was apparently to be bought off, possibly by presenting her with Asia. Germany suddenly came to the conclusion that she might never again have such a favorable opportunity for this final war. Russia and France would increase in military power at her expense faster than she would increase in naval power at England's expense. Russia appeared to be in the throes of revolution, England unable to avert a civil war. France had forgotten to keep her powder dry and was in a state of financial chaos. Therefore she determined that Russia should lose power by submitting to humiliation, or if she refused to do this, France should be smothered by a military avalanche before Russia had time to mobilize. For English Governments Germany had such a contempt that she did not believe that any British Premier would declare war, however suicidal it might be for England to stand by, waiting to be extinguished when other nations were in the dust.

Did Austria receive her orders from the Kaiser, who proceeded to throw dust into the eyes of Europe until the psychological moment should arrive ?

The war has severed us from the rest of the world, all our cable communications are destroyed. But the winds will carry the mighty voice of Justice even across the ocean. We trust in God, we have confidence in the judgment of right-minded men. And through the roar of battle we call to you all. Do not believe the mischievous lies that our enemies are spreading about. We do not know if victory will be ours, the Lord alone knows. We have not chosen our path, we must continue doing our duty, even to the very end. We bear the misery of war, the death of our sons, believing in Germany, believing in duty.

> " The war has severed us from the rest of the world, all our cable communications are destroyed. But the winds will carry the mighty voice of Justice even across the ocean. " With reference to this one is bound to remark that whatever the mighty voice of Justice has to say about the matter—and the world does not think that its verdict is for the Kaiser, the wanton destroyer of Joan of Arc's Cathedral of Rheims—the winds must have been the medium through which " Count John Bernstorff, " the German Ambassador in the United States, has received the war news with which he has been favoring the United States papers. The wind also takes German news to the Turkish and South American papers daily.

And we know that Germany cannot be wiped from the face of the earth.

"Germany cannot be wiped from the face of the earth." Every sane man knows that; every sane man is glad of it. The quarrel of the world is not with Germany, which has done so much for music and scholarship, art, and science. It is German militarism which all mankind outside of Germany—and a good deal of the mankind within its limits—desires to see wiped out.

FOREWORD TO CHAPTER II

By Robert Blatchford in the *Daily Mail*, August 25th, 1914.

"This is not a royal war, nor a Government war, nor a war of diplomatic making; it is a war of free nations against a devilish system of imperial domination and national spoliation. There can be no security in Europe until Germany is defeated."

"The fact is we have stood by France and Belgium in this war because our national existence depended upon them."

"And now Britain and her Allies must beat Germany or Germany will beat them."

"This war did not originate in the murder of the Austrian Grand Duke. It arose out of the German desire to dominate the world. It is not a casual war, caused by some offense of yesterday; it is a deliberate war of aggression, for which German ambition has been arming and preparing for more than twenty years.

"This war did not spring up suddenly because a Servian fanatic threw a bomb. Its seed was sown by the Prussian military writer Clausewitz, the master of Bismarck. Since Prussia adopted the policies and strategy of Clausewitz this war has been coming. The Prussian attack on Denmark in 1864, upon Austria in 1866, and upon France in 1870, were steps towards this war; the building of the German fleet, the fortification of Heligoland, the making of the Kiel Canal, the increase in the German Army, the imposition of the great German war tax of fifty millions, the construction of strategic railways to the Belgian border—all these were steps towards this war.

"We could not keep out of this war because, had we been so

15

cowardly as to desert the Belgians and the French, we should have
had to fight Germany afterwards, and without allies."

Article from *Die Wahrheit*, August 5, quoted by the *Times*,
22d August, 1914.

"'From the first moment of the war, from every big and small
aspect of the present sanguinary conflict, justice and civilization
went against the Kaiser, and he has on his side only brutal and
inhuman force and violence.

"'The ultimatum of Austria to Servia was a brutal demand of
a Great Power to a small country. The Kaiser's demand that
Russia should not spoil Austria's sanguinary meal in Servia was
both unjust and stupid. The most terrible act, however, was the
Kaiser's declaration of war against Belgium. Such an act sets
mankind again on the road to the days of barbarity and cannibal-
ism. As for England, she fights in this war not for her present
existence, but for her future existence, not for to-day, but for
to-morrow. England knows, and the whole world knows, that a
victorious Germany against all countries engaged in the war
would lead to the political end of England.'"

Article in the *American Hebrew* of New York, quoted by the *Times*,
22d August, 1914.

"'After forty-five years of peace Germany breaks its record,
and plunges into war which not one of its defenders can fairly
justify. It is criminal aggression and nothing else which led
Germany to turn about, violate the neutrality of Belgium, and
force its way into France. The campaign was clearly planned
before the ultimatum was issued to Russia. The Kaiser will go
down into history as the most patient War Lord that ever lived.
He waited and waited, and then selected the most inopportune
and unjustifiable occasion to plunge his country into war. The
world is on the brink of universal disaster. A madman in
Europe moves and disturbs the "balance of power."'"

CHAPTER II

HOW THE WAR CAME ABOUT

WHO IS RESPONSIBLE FOR THE WAR?—NOT GER-
MANY!—ENGLAND'S POLICY!—HER SHIFTING
OF RESPONSIBILITY AND PROMOTING THE
STRUGGLE WHILE ALONE POSSESSING POWER
TO AVERT IT!

THE pamphlet accuses England of being responsible for the war, of promoting it while
she alone could avert it, and ingenuously proceeds
to remark that " the very parties and persons who
wanted the war, either at once or later, assert
that the enemy wanted and began it." No one
will dispute the judgment of the pamphlet in this
matter.

It is an old and common experience that after the
outbreak of a war the very parties and persons
that wanted the war, either at once or later, assert
that the enemy wanted and began it. The German Empire especially always had to suffer from
such untruthful assertions, and the very first days
of the present terrible European war confirm this
old experience. Again Russian, French, and
British accounts represent the German Empire
as having wanted the war.

It is unreasonable to suppose that Russia or
France wanted the war when the pamphlet itself
points out that Russia and France in two years'
time would be so powerful that they would
always be reminding the world that they were
invincible (see page 125). And it was really very
ingenuous of Germany to force England into a
war with her at a moment when our perfidious
nation had the support of three other first-class
Powers, instead of politely waiting till Germany
could take her alone at a moment of the most
complete disadvantage.

Only a few months ago influential men and
newspapers of Great Britain as well as of Paris
could be heard to express the opinion that nobody
in Europe wanted war and that especially the
German Emperor and his Government had sincerely and effectively been working for peace.
Especially the English Government in the course
of the last two years asserted frequently and
publicly, and was supported by the *Westminster
Gazette* and a number of influential English newspapers in the assertion, that Great Britain and
the German Empire during the Balkan crisis of
the last few years had always met on the same
platform for the preservation of peace.

There is no doubt that during the Balkan war
the German Emperor and Government did
sincerely and effectively work for peace. But I
do not see why the pamphlet emphasizes this,
for it only serves to emphasize the fact that the
present war would have been averted if Germany

had sincerely worked for peace. It leads us to the irresistible conclusion that the Germans worked for peace in the Balkan war because their expectations as to its course had not been realized. Instead of destroying the power of the Slav States banded against Turkey, it showed (1) that if a European war happened then, Russia and the Balkan nations would eat up Austria in a month, and be face to face with Germany, and (2) it gave Germany the hint of which she has taken such brilliant advantage—that her artillery needed overhauling, since the Turkish Krupps were entirely outclassed by the French guns of the Allies. It was much more advantageous to Germany that Austria should rob both Greece and Servia of the fruits of their victories, which they expected on the Adriatic, and should inspire Bulgaria to wreck the Balkan League, which had proved so inconveniently powerful. It is not to be forgotten that the King of Bulgaria is a prince with Austrian connections.

The late Secretary of State, von Kiderlen-Waechter, his successor, Mr. von Jagow, and the Imperial Chancellor, von Bethmann-Hollweg, likewise declared repeatedly in the Reichstag how great their satisfaction was that a close and confidential diplomatic coöperation with Great Britain, especially in questions concerning the near East, had become a fact. And it has to be acknowledged to-day that at that time the German and British interests in the near East were identical, or at any rate ran in parallel lines.

There has undoubtedly been a disposition in recent years for Great Britain and Germany to be more conciliatory to each other on Eastern questions. The pity was that at a critical moment the wisdom of Germany's statesmen went for nothing. The war party was strong enough to sweep them aside.

The collapse of European Turkey in the war against the Balkan alliance created an entirely new situation. At first Bulgaria was victorious and great, then it was beaten and humiliated by the others with the intellectual help of Russia.

Bulgaria was involved in war with the other Balkan powers by the machinations of Austria. The strength of the Balkan League threw a power as strong as Austria into the balance of Europe on the Russian side. To suppose that Russia took any part in breaking it up, as this pamphlet suggests, is sheer imbecility. To Austria, on the other hand, it was a matter of life and death to break up the League, and Bulgaria was so arrogant and so greedy that it was easy to seduce her.

There could be no doubt about Russia's intentions: she was preparing for the total subjection of weakened Turkey and for taking possession of the Dardanelles and Constantinople in order to rule from this powerful position Turkey and the other Balkan states. Great Britain and the German Empire, which only had economic interests in Turkey, were bound to wish to strengthen

Turkey besides trying to prevent the Moscovite rule on the whole Balkan peninsula.

> It follows that if Russia had had any idea of proceeding to acquire the Dardanelles and Constantinople, she would have preserved the Balkan League by every means in her power to incapacitate Austria from objecting. It is curious, too, if this was the aim of Russia, that she has shown no sign whatever of a design to take the Dardanelles or Constantinople.

Servia had come out of the second Balkan war greatly strengthened, and with her territory very much increased. Russia had done everything to strengthen this bitter enemy of our ally Austria-Hungary. For a great number of years Servian politicians and conspirators had planned to undermine the southeastern provinces of Austria-Hungary, and, to separate them from the dual monarchy.

> Undoubtedly Servia had come out of her two wars greatly strengthened as well as greatly increased in size. Undoubtedly Russia wished her well, and had with difficulty restrained Slav feeling when Servia was deprived of half the fruits of her victories by Austria's denying her access to the sea. Undoubtedly Greece was also angry with Austria for checking her Albanian aspirations. And Austria's protégée and dupe, Bulgaria, had extinguished herself for the time being. It is equally certain that Servia owed Austria another

grudge for seizing Bosnia and the Herzegovina, and made herself the center of the aspirations of the various Serb peoples, in Austria as well as Servia, to be united in a greater Servia, just as the Italians of Lombardy and Venetia were freed from Austria and united to the rest of Italy half a century ago. But it is more than doubtful if Russia had given Servia the smallest encouragement to begin active operations in any way. The Germans themselves acted on the belief that Russia would not be ready to fight till 1916. Had the Balkan League survived, the case would have been different; but Austria had checkmated this first move.

In Servia as well as in Russia prevailed the opinion that, at the first attack, Austria-Hungary would fall to pieces. In this case, Servia was to receive South Austria and Russia was to dictate the peace in Vienna. The Balkan war had ruined Turkey almost entirely, had paralyzed Bulgaria, that was friendly, and had strengthened the Balkan states that were hostile to Austria. At the same time there began in Roumania a Russian and French propaganda, that promised this country, if it should join the dual alliance, the Hungarian province of Siebenbuergen.

The world may shortly know if Roumania has been promised, and has accepted, a Hungarian province as the price of joining the Triple Entente.

Thus it became evident in Germany and in Austria that at St. Petersburg first by diplomatic and political, then also by military action, a comprehensive attack of Slavism under Russian guidance was being prepared.   The party of the Grand Dukes in St. Petersburg, the party of the Russian officers, always ready for war, and the Panslavists, the brutal and unscrupulous representatives of the idea that the Russian czarism was destined to rule Europe—all these declared openly that their aim was the destruction of Austria-Hungary.

If the Russian Grand Dukes' military party and Panslavists have openly declared that their aim was the destruction of Austria-Hungary, the British Press has not thought the fate of Austria-Hungary of sufficient importance to chronicle these declarations. But the statement is absolutely untrue. Not the slightest proof of it has been offered.

In Russia the army, already of an immense size, was increased secretly but comprehensively and as quick as possible; in Servia the same was done, and the Russian Ambassador in Belgrade, Mr. v. Hartwig, was, after the second Balkan war, the principal promoter of the plan to form against Austria a new Balkan alliance.

For the first time I find myself in complete agreement with the editors of the pamphlet. I have no doubt that the Russian army was being increased as comprehensively, as quickly, and as secretly as possible, and that the Russian Ambassador in Belgrade, von Hartwig, was doing

his best to form a new Balkan alliance against Austria.

In Bosnia during all this time the Servian propaganda was at work with high treason, and in the end with the revolver and the bomb.

In Vienna and in Berlin the greatness and the purpose of the new danger could not remain doubtful, especially as it was openly said in St. Petersburg, in Belgrade, and elsewhere that the destruction of Austria-Hungary was imminent.

> **Doubtless the Servian agitation was being briskly maintained, but it is admitted now that the murders of the Archduke and his wife were due to Bosnian revenge. One of the assassins had, in fact, previously been described by Austria to Servia as a " harmless individual." (See English White Paper.) It is the tradition of the Austrians to behave infamously to their subject-races. The imminence of the dissolution of the Hapsburg Empire is one of the most intelligent forecasts in the book.**

As soon as the Balkan troubles began, Austria-Hungary had been obliged to put a large part of her army in readiness for war, because the Russians and Servians had mobilized on their frontiers. The Germans felt that what was a danger for their ally was also a danger for them, and that they must do all in their power to maintain Austria-Hungary in the position of a great power. They felt that this could only be done by keeping with their ally perfect faith and by great military strength, so that Russia might possibly be deterred from war and peace be preserved, or else, that in case war was forced upon them, that they could wage it with honor and success.

> During the Balkan war Austria-Hungary had been obliged to keep a number of men under arms, because Russia had felt compelled to do so, and Servia was, of course, one of the combatants. One can understand that Germany on her part had to keep herself so ready for war that Russia might be deterred from it. But she was anxious not to be drawn into it herself. The time was not ripe.

Now it was clear in Berlin that in view of the Russian and Servian preparations Austria-Hungary in case of a war would be obliged to use a great part of her forces against Servia, and therefore would have to send against Russia fewer troops than would have been possible under the conditions formerly prevailing in Europe. Formerly, even European Turkey could have been counted upon for assistance, that after her recent defeat seemed very doubtful. These reasons and considerations which were solely of a *defensive* nature led to the great German military bills of the last two years. Also Austria-Hungary was obliged to increase its defensive strength.

> It may be conceded that the reason why Germany has increased her military strength so much

during the last two years is partly due to the fact that Austria would be obliged to use so much of her forces against Servia that she is no longer a balance against Russia.   Much more was it due to the fact that Turkey, whom Germany reckoned as a member of the Triple All ance, had been seriously crippled.

Whoever considers carefully the course of events that has been sketched here, will pronounce the assertions of our enemies that Germany wanted the war, ridiculous and absurd.   On the contrary, it can be said that Germany never before endeavored more eagerly to preserve peace than during the last few years.   Germany had plenty of opportunities to attack and good opportunities to boot, for we knew for years that the army of France was no more ready than that of Russia.

The assertion that Germany wanted the war is not ridiculous and absurd.   We have plenty of reasons for knowing that Germany not only wanted war, but meant to have it.   During the past year she had imported vast quantities of wheat from Canada.   She had uniforms ready of the new field-service gray for four million men the moment they were called to the colors, and she had raised far more than the fifty millions intended from the special levy on property.   The fact that she had not attacked the Allies before this, in spite of the knowledge that they were not ready, is not conclusive.   If they were not ready, neither was her fleet, and she was waiting for the minute when circumstances would be more against them.   In France, for instance, there was a tendency in politics which boded ill for keeping up military preparations, as was shown in her difficulties over forming Governments in the past year.

The teachings of von Bernhardl in his " Germany and the Next War," and similar writers, added to the behavior of the Emperor in the present crisis, seem to prove that his reiterated assertion that the preservation of peace was his principal aim was accompanied by the mental reservation until the moment that Germany could snatch an advantage by breaking it.

But the Germans are not a warlike nation, and the German Emperor, with his government, has always shown how earnestly he meant his reiterated assertions, that the preservation of peace was his principal aim.   He was actuated in this by the general consideration of humanity, justice, and culture, as well as by the consideration of German trade and commerce.   This, especially the trans-oceanic commerce of Germany, has increased from year to year.   War, however, means the ruin of commerce.   Why expose Germany needlessly to this terrible risk, especially as everything in Germany prospered and her wealth increased?

In addition to the pleasure of being considered a humane, just and cultured sovereign, he was doubtless moved by the consideration of German trade and commerce. These were increasing by leaps and bounds, and war, as the book sententiously observes, means the ruin of commerce. There was every reason why he should not expose Germany to these terrible risks until he saw his enemies in a quagmire and had only to shoot them down. The presentation of the veiled ultimatum to Russia in 1909, and Germany's behavior over the Agadir crisis in 1911, are a sufficient comment on Germany's love of peace.

No, the German army bills were merely meant to protect us against, and prepare us for, the attacks of Moscovite barbarism. But nobody in Germany has ever doubted for a moment that France would attack us at the first Russian signal. Since the first days of the Franco-Russian alliance things have become entirely reversed: *Then* France wanted to win Russia for a war of revenge against Germany; *now*, on the contrary, France thought herself obliged to place her power and her existence at the disposal of the Russian lust of conquest.

Undoubtedly the last increase in the German army would not have been necessary had it not been for the collapse of Turkey, whom she regarded as a member of the Triple Alliance and the increasing military power of Russia, labelled by the book " Moscovite barbarism," though doubtless the Belgians would have preferred it to German civilization. Though the case is stated disingenuously, doubtless if Germany was attacked, it would be from the Russian frontier, not because France formerly wanted to win Russia for a war of revenge and had now ceased to do so, but, out of gratitude, thought herself under an obligation to place her power and her existence at the disposal of the Russian lust of conquest, but because France was likely at all times to want peace, and Russia, having grown immensely stronger since she was humiliated by Germany in 1909, was likely to strike the bully at the first attempt to renew the provocation.

The weak link in the chain of reasoning is that there is no sort of proof either in this pamphlet or elsewhere that France and Russia had any scheme for attacking Germany.

In the spring of 1914 the German press reported from St. Petersburg detailed accounts of Russia's comprehensive preparations for war. They were not denied in Russia, and Paris declared that Russia would be ready in two or three years and then pursue a policy corresponding to her power; France, too, would then be at the height of her power. If the German Government had desired war, on the strength of these accounts, *which were true*, it could have waged a preventive war at once and easily. It did not do so, considering that a war is just only when it is forced upon one by the enemy. Thus spring went by with the atmosphere at high tension. From St. Petersburg and Paris overbearing threats came in increasing numbers to the effect that the power of the Dual Alliance was now gigantic and that Germany and Austria soon would begin to feel it. We remained quiet and watchful, endeavoring with perseverance and with all our might to win over Great Britain to the policy of preserving peace. Colonial and economic questions were being discussed by the German and English Governments, and the cordiality between the two great Powers seemed only to be equalled by their mutual confidence.

Here we have a frank declaration. " A war is just only when it is forced upon one by the enemy." Clearly, then, Germany cannot regard this war as just, for so far from being forced upon her, she forced it on Russia, who had actually come to an amicable agreement with Austria.

This is an ingenuous confession of Germany that she had, owing to the alarming reports of her military attaché in Russia, known since the spring that she must strike now if she was not to lose the advantage she had gained in military power by the fresh additions she had made to her army with the 1913 levy of fifty millions on hitherto untaxed sources (on capital instead of income). This fifty millions, or possibly more, had brought Germany to the height of her possible military power, and the other countries, though they had tried to take corresponding steps to increase their power, had not yet obtained full value out of them. Therefore, Germany's chance had come.

For a few months Germany delayed having " a quarrel forced on her by the enemy "— in this

instance it was Russia from whom she desired a
"casus belli," while she was endeavoring to
detach Great Britain from the Triple Entente.
Having this in her mind, her relations with
Britain on Colonial and other questions were
more cordial than they had been for a long time
past. In July, Germany either considered that she
had achieved her end with Great Britain or that it
never would be achieved (probably the former,
as she was very badly served by her diplomats
throughout), and inspired Austria's ultimatum to
Servia. At any rate, she knew that Great Britain
would sympathize with Austria over the constant
pin-pricks and provocation which she had received from Servia, and that, if it could be made
to appear that the war was all concerning Servia,
the British Government would find the country
very difficult to move. The famous poster of
"John Bull"—"To Hell with Servia!"—voiced
the sentiment of the country before the whole of
the situation was understood. The murder of the
Archduke Francis Ferdinand and his wife gave
the War-party in Germany the chance they
wanted. Without it they might have tried to
make some other incident, but would probably
not have succeeded.

Then on the 28th of June occurred that fright-
ful assassination by Servians of the successor to
the Austro-Hungarian throne, Archduke Francis
Ferdinand.

All the civilized world sympathized with Austria after the dastardly murder of the Archduke,

who lost his life by a truly imperial intrepidity. But it was admitted later, that it was the work of Bosnians, who had been forced to become subjects of Austria against their will, AND NOT SERVIANS.

The Greater-Servia propaganda of action had put aside the man who was especially hated in Servia as the powerful exponent of Austro-Hungarian unity and strength. This murder is the real cause of the present European war. Austria-Hungary was able to prove to a shuddering world a few days after the murder, that it had been prepared and planned systematically, yea, that the Servian Government had been cognizant of the plan.

> The murder of the Archduke Francis Ferdinand and his wife was not the real cause of the present war. There is nothing to show that the Servian Government was concerned in it in the smallest degree; it was the result of the annexation of Bosnia and the Herzegovina five years before. Although the bomb came from Servia, because it was not easy for the murderers to obtain their materials on Austrian soil, the murder was primarily an act of revenge for Austrian oppression of its Slav subjects, however it developed politically. It would be almost as reasonable to assert that the murder was engineered by Germany in order to have European opinion on the side of the Teutonic Alliance in the war which they were about to start. General von Bernhardi would be quite capable of coining one of his admirable

epigrams to show that this was what a modern
Machiavelli was bound to advise. The murder
was not the cause of the war; whoever planned
it, Germany seized upon it as a heaven-sent
justification.

The immense extent of the Servian revolutionary organization in the provinces of Southern
Austria, the warlike spirit of the Servians and its
instigation by Russia and France imposed upon
the Vienna Government the duty to insist upon
quiet and peace within and without its borders.

No reasonable man could say that it may not
have been necessary for Austria to insist on a
definite cessation of the Servian revolutionary
organization in its southern provinces, backed as
it was by the great military qualities of the Servian nation on its borders. It cannot have been
instigated by Russia, much less by France, or
Russia would not have pressed Servia to submit
to Austria's unconscionably unreasonable demands when it was quite certain that Austria
could not reduce the Switzerland of the Balkans
without many months of fighting and a battle or
two of the kind which sent her flying out of Servia
in August.

It addressed to the Servian Government a
number of demands which aimed at nothing but
the suppression of the anti-Austrian propaganda.

A perusal of the ultimatum addressed by Austria to the Servian Government will not confirm
this view.

3

AUSTRIA'S ULTIMATUM TO SERVIA

"To achieve this end the Imperial and Royal Government sees itself compelled to demand from the Royal Servian Government a formal assurance that it condemns this dangerous propaganda against the Monarchy; in other words, the whole series of tendencies, the ultimate aim of which is to detach from the Monarchy territories belonging to it, and that it undertakes to suppress by every means this criminal and terrorist propaganda.

"In order to give a formal character to this undertaking the Royal Servian Government shall publish on the front page of its 'Official Journal' of the 26th June (13th July), the following declaration:

"'The Royal Government of Servia condemns the propaganda directed against Austria-Hungary—i. e., the general tendency of which the final aim is to detach from the Austro-Hungarian Monarchy territories belonging to it, and it sincerely deplores the fatal consequence of these criminal proceedings.

"'The Royal Government regrets that Servian officers and functionaries participated in the above-mentioned pro-

THE SERVIAN REPLY

"The Royal Government has received the notification of the Austro-Hungarian Government of the 10th inst., and is convinced that its answer will remove every misunderstanding that threatens to disturb the pleasant neighborly relations between the Austro-Hungarian Monarchy and the Servian Kingdom.

"The Royal Goverament is certain that in dealing with the great neighboring monarchy these protests have under no pretexts been renewed which formerly were made both in the Skupshtina and in explanations and negotiations of responsible representatives of the State, and which, through the declaration of the Servian Government of March 18th, 1909, were settled; furthermore, that since that time none of the various successive Governments of the kingdom, nor any of its officers, has made an attempt to change the political and legal conditions set up in Bosnia and Herzegovina. The Royal Government is certain that the Austro-Hungarian Government has made no representations of any kind along this line except in the case of a textbook concern-

paganda, and thus compromised the good neighborly relations to which the Royal Government was solemnly pledged by its declaration of the 31st March, 1909.

"'The Royal Government, which disapproves and repudiates all idea of interfering or attempting to interfere with the destinies of the inhabitants of any part whatsoever of Austria-Hungary, considers it its duty formally to warn officers and functionaries, and the whole population of the kingdom, that henceforward it will proceed with the utmost rigor against persons who may be guilty of such machinations, which it will use all its efforts to anticipate and suppress.'

"This declaration shall simultaneously be communicated to the Royal Army as an order of the day by His Majesty the King and shall be published in the 'Official Bulletin' of the Army.

ing which the Austro-Hungarian Government received an entirely satisfactory reply. Servia, during the Balkan crisis, gave evidence in numerous cases of her pacific and temperate policies, and it will be thanks to Servia alone and the sacrifices that she alone made in the interest of European peace if that peace continue.

"The Royal Government cannot be held responsible for utterances of a private character such as newspaper articles and the peaceful work of societies, utterances which are quite ordinary in almost all countries, and which are not generally under State control, especially since the Royal Government, in the solution of a great number of questions that came up between Servia and Austria-Hungary, showed much consideration as a result of which most of these questions were settled in the best interests of the progress of the two neighboring countries.

"The Royal Government was therefore painfully surprised to hear the contention that Servian subjects had taken part in the preparations for the murder committed in Serajevo. It had hoped to be invited to coöperate in the investigations following this crime, and was prepared, in order to prove the entire correctness of its acts, to proceed against all persons concerning whom it had received information.

"In conformity with the wish of the Austro-Hungarian Government, the Royal Government is prepared to turn over to the court, regardless of station or rank, any Servian subject concerning whose participation in the crime at Serajevo proofs may be given to it. The Government pledges itself especially to publish on the first page of the official organ of July 26th the following declaration:

"'The Royal Servian Government condemns every propaganda that may be directed against Austria-Hungary; that is to say, all efforts designed ultimately to sever territory from the Austro-Hungarian Monarchy, and it regrets sincerely the sad consequences of these criminal machinations.'

"The Royal Government regrets that, in accordance with advices from the Austro-Hungarian Government, certain Servian officers and functionaries are taking an active part in the present propaganda, and that they have thereby jeopardized the pleasant neighborly relations to the maintenance of which the Royal Government was formally pledged by the declaration of March 31st, 1909.

"The Government (what follows here is similar to the text demanded).

"The Royal Servian Government further undertakes:

"The Royal Government further pledges itself:

"1. To suppress any publication which incites to hatred and contempt of the Austro-Hungarian Monarchy and the general tendency of which is directed against its territorial integrity;

"1. To introduce a provision in the press law on the occasion of the next regular session of the Skupshtina, according to which instigations to hatred and contempt of the Austro-Hungarian Monarchy, as well as any publication directed in general against the territorial integrity of Austria-Hungary, shall be punished severely.

"The Government pledges itself, on the occasion of the coming revision of the Constitution, to add to Article XXII. a clause permitting the confiscation of publications, the confiscation of which, under the present Article XXII. of the Constitution, would be impossible.

"2. To dissolve immediately the society styled Narodna Odbrana, to confiscate all its means of propaganda, and to proceed in the same manner against other societies and their branches in Servia which engage in propaganda against

"2. The Government possesses no proof—and the Note of the Austro-Hungarian Government provides it with none —that the 'Narodna Odbrana' Society and other similar associations have up to the present committed any criminal acts

the Austro-Hungarian Monarchy. The Royal Government shall take the necessary measures to prevent the societies dissolved from continuing their activity under another name and form;

"3. To eliminate without delay from public instruction in Servia, both as regards the teaching body and also as regards the methods of instruction, everything that serves, or might serve, to foment the propaganda against Austria-Hungary;

"4. To remove from the military service, and from the administration in general, all officers and functionaries guilty of propaganda against the Austro-Hungarian Monarchy whose names and deeds the Austro-Hungarian Government reserves to itself the right of communicating to the Royal Government;

"5. To accept the collaboration in Servia of representatives of the Austro-Hungarian Government in the suppression of the subversive movement

through any of their members. Nevertheless, the Royal Government will accept the demand of the Austro-Hungarian Government and dissolve the Narodna Odbrana Society, as well as all societies that may work against Austria-Hungary.

"3. The Royal Servian Government agrees to eliminate forthwith from public education in Servia everything that might help the propaganda against Austria-Hungary, provided that the Austro-Hungarian Government gives it actual proof of this propaganda.

"4. The Royal Government is also ready to discharge from military and civil service such officers—provided it is proved against them by legal investigation—who have implicated themselves in acts directed against the territorial integrity of the Austro-Hungarian Monarchy; the Government expects that, for the purpose of instituting proceedings, the Austro-Hungarian Government will impart the names of these officers and employés and the acts of which they are accused.

"5. The Royal Servian Government must confess that it is not quite clear as to the sense and scope of the desire of the Austro-Hungarian Government to the effect that the

directed against the territorial integrity of the Monarchy;

"6. To take judicial proceedings against accessories to the plot of the 28th June who are on Servian territory. Delegates of the Austro-Hungarian Government will take part in the investigation relating thereto;

"7. To proceed without delay to the arrest of Major Voija Tankositch and of the individual named Milan Ciganovitch, a Servian State employé, who have been compromised by the results of the magisterial enquiry at Serajevo;

Royal Servian Government bind itself to allow the coöperation within its territory of representatives of the Austro-Hungarian Government, but it nevertheless declares itself willing to permit such coöperation as might be in conformity with international law and criminal procedure, as well as with friendly neighborly relations.

"6. The Royal Government naturally holds itself bound to institute an investigation against all such persons as were concerned in the plot of June 15th–28th, or are supposed to have been concerned in it, and are on Servian soil. As to the coöperation of special delegates of the Austro-Hungarian Government in this investigation, the Servian Government cannot accept such coöperation, since this would be a violation of the laws and criminal procedure. However, in individual cases, information as to the progress of the investigation might be given to the Austro-Hungarian delegates.

"7. On the very evening on which your Note arrived the Royal Government caused the arrest of Major Voislar Tankosic. But, regarding Milan Ciganovic, who is a subject of the Austro-Hungarian Monarchy, and who was employed until June 15th (as candidate) in the Department of Railroads it has not been possible to arrest this man up till now, for which reason a warrant has been issued against him.

"The Austro-Hungarian Government is requested, in order that the investigation may be made as soon as possible, to make known in the specified form what grounds of suspicion exist, and the proofs of guilt collected at the investigation in Serajevo.

"8. To prevent by effective measures the coöperation of the Servian authorities in the illicit traffic in arms and explosives across the frontier, to dismiss and punish severely the officials of the frontier service at Schabatz and Loznica guilty of having assisted the perpetrators of the Serajevo crime by facilitating their passage across the frontier;

"8. The Servian Government will increase the severity and scope of its measures against the smuggling of arms and explosives.

"It goes without saying that it will at once start an investigation and mete out severe punishment to the frontier officials of the Sabac-Loznica line who failed in their duty and allowed those responsible for the crime to cross the frontier.

"9. To furnish the Imperial and Royal Government with explanations regarding the unjustifiable utterances of high Servian officials, both in Servia and abroad, who, notwithstanding their official position, did not hesitate after the crime of the 28th June to express themselves in interviews in terms of hostility to

"9. The Royal Government is willing to give explanations of the statements made in interviews by its officials in Servia and foreign countries after the crime, and which, according to the Austro-Hungarian Government, were anti-Austrian, as soon as the said Government indicates where these statements were made,

the Austro-Hungarian Government; and finally,

"10. To notify the Imperial and Royal Government without delay of the execution of the measures comprised under the preceding heads.

and provides proofs that such statements were actually made by the said officials. The Royal Government will itself take steps to collect the necessary proofs and means of transmission for this purpose.

"10. The Royal Government will, in so far as this has not already occurred in this Note, inform the Austro-Hungarian Government of the taking of the measures concerning the foregoing matters, as soon as such measures have been ordered and carried out.

"The Royal Servian Government is of the opinion that it is mutually advantageous not to hinder the settlement of this question, and therefore, in case the Austro-Hungarian Government should not consider itself satisfied with this answer, it is ready as always to accept a peaceful solution, either by referring the decision of this question to the international tribunal at The Hague, or by leaving it to the great Powers who coöperated in the preparation of the explanation given by the Servian Government on the 17th-31st March, 1909."

"The Austro-Hungarian Government expects the reply of the Royal Government at the latest by six o'clock on Saturday evening, the 25th July."

In the afternoon of July 25th Mr. Crackanthorpe, the British Representative in Servia, telegraphed:

"Belgrade,
"July 25th, 1914.
"The Council of Ministers are now drawing up their reply to

the Austrian Note. I am informed by the Under-Secretary of
State for Foreign Affairs that it will be most conciliatory and will
meet the Austrian demands in as large a measure as is possible.
  "The following is a brief summary of the projected reply:
  "'The Servian Government consent to the publication of a
declaration in the *Official Gazette*. The ten points are accepted
with reservations. Servian Government declares themselves
ready to agree to a mixed commission of enquiry so long as the
appointment of the commission can be shown to be in accordance
with international usage. They consent to dismiss and prosecute those officers who can be clearly proved to be guilty, and they
have already arrested the officer referred to in the Austrian Note.
They are prepared to suppress the Narodna Odbrana.
  "'The Servian Government consider that, unless the Austrian
Government want war at any cost, they cannot but be content
with the full satisfaction offered in the Servian reply.'"

  In the evening, as the Austrian Note had not been agreed to
unconditionally, he had to supplement his first telegram with the
following ominous message:

"Belgrade,
  "July 25th, 1914.

  "The Austrian Minister left at 6.30.
  "The Government has left for Nish, where the Skupshtina
will meet on Monday. I am leaving with my other colleagues,
but the Vice-Consul is remaining in charge of the archives."

  Servia was on the point of accepting the demand,
when there arrived a dispatch from St. Petersburg
and Servia mobilized. Then Austria, too, had
to act. Thus arose the Austro-Servian war.

  To say that Servia was on the point of accepting
the demands of Austria when she had a dispatch
from St. Petersburg and mobilized instead, is one
of the most deliberate misstatements in a book
which is rich in them. Russia, as this book itself

has emphasized, had every reason for desiring that there should be no war till 1916, when her siege artillery for smashing up German fortresses would be ready. In the face of this, it is not necessary to adduce the incontrovertible evidence of the Czar's love of peace. Also, all the world knows what strong pressure Russia brought to bear on Servia to make her compose her quarrel with Austria. "Then Austria, too, had to act," says this veracious book. "Thus arose the Austro-Servian war." Austria, as Mr. Crackanthorpe's dispatch, quoted on the preceding page, shows, meant the war with Servia to take place immediately and irrevocably. Otherwise she would not have addressed to Servia an ultimatum so almost impossible of acceptance by a high-spirited and powerful nation—an ultimatum, moreover, to which submission had to be made within forty-eight hours. The chivalrous and peace-loving Count Berchtold, to whom Europe owed so much during the Balkan war, let the cat out of the bag about this when he said that the remonstrances of England came too late. Why did they come too late? Austria knew that England would take this line the moment the matter came to her ears, and could have laid the matter before her as much earlier as she chose. The remonstrance came too late because Austria intended it to come too late. In all human probability that phrase, signed by the unwilling hand of Austria's Foreign Minister, was the death-warrant of the Empire of the Habsburgs.

It is plain that Austria wished to present Europe with a "fait accompli."

But a few days later, the Russian army was being mobilized, and the mobilization was begun also in France.   At the same time, as the German White-Book clearly proves, the diplomacy of Russia and France asserted its great love of peace and tried to prolong the negotiations in order to gain time, for, as is well known, the Russian mobilization proceeds slowly.   Germany was waiting, and again and again the German Emperor tried to win the Czar over to the preservation of peace, for he considered him sincere, and thought him his personal friend.   Emperor William was to be cruelly disappointed.   He finally saw himself obliged to proclaim the state of war for Germany.

> Germany seems to have been anxious, before her brief connection with China was extinguished, to try her hand at Chinese diplomacy. "A few days later," says this book, "the Russian army was being mobilized, and mobilization was begun also in France."   This was absolutely untrue as regards France.   "The diplomacy of Russia and France asserted its great love of peace, and tried to prolong the negotiations . . . to gain time. . . .   The Russian mobilization proceeds slowly."
>
> The committee, who produced this book, are well aware that at any moment one word from the German Emperor would have brought Austria to a full-stop.   France was not mobilizing, and did not mobilize till a matter of hours before the war.   The Kaiser knew that Russia would mobilize unless she could be bluffed into submission.

He was guilty of playing with the peace of Europe as if it had been a hand at poker.

The Kaiser complains of the behavior of the Czar. There was once a political play presented at the Criterion Theater, in which a very militant Mr. Arthur Bourchier complained of being hectored by a very pacific Mr. Weedon Grossmith. " Wild horses would not persuade me," said Mr. Bourchier. " Am I those wild horses?" asked Mr. Grossmith. When his bluff failed, the Kaiser wept crocodile's tears and proclaimed a " state of war " for Germany, which is the code word for mobilization. The damning and conclusive answer to this piece of hypocrisy is the revelation of Sir Maurice de Bunsen that the German ultimatum to Russia was presented " after " Austria had given way and accepted the Russian demands.

But at that time the Russian and French armies were already in a state of complete mobilization.

As has been shown, the French army was not mobilized, nor were its mobilization arrangements at all perfect. Russia had mobilized upon the Austrian frontier, having divined that nothing but panic would stop the thick-headed Austrians from proceeding with the campaign against Servia which they had promised themselves.

At that time the London *Daily Graphic* wrote the following article, which shows how an English paper that was only slightly friendly to Germany judged of the situation at the time:

" THE MOBILIZATION MYSTERY.

"A general mobilization has been ordered in Russia, and Germany has responded by proclaiming martial law throughout the Empire. We are now enabled to measure exactly the narrow and slippery ledge which still stands between Europe and the abyss of Armageddon. Will the Russian order be acted upon in the provinces adjoining the German frontier? If it is, then the work of the peacemakers is at an end, for Germany is bound to reply with a mobilization of her own armed force, and a rush to the frontiers on all sides must ensue. We confess that we are unable to understand the action of Russia in view of the resumption of the negotiations with Austria. It is not likely that these negotiations have been resumed unless both sides think that there is yet a chance of agreement, but if this is the case, why the mobilization which goes far beyond the limits of necessary precaution, and is, indeed, calculated to defeat the efforts of the diplomatists, however promising they may be? There may, of course, be a satisfactory explanation, but as the matter stands, it is inexplicable, and is all the more regrettable because it is calculated—we feel sure unjustly—to cast doubts on the loyalty and straightforwardness of the Russian Government."

The " Daily Graphic " was the only paper, outside of the Ostrich Press, which loves to bury its head in the sand when war is on the horizon, which questioned Russia's right to mobilize. Russia mobilized to save the peace of Europe. There was not the smallest doubt that if she refused to be humiliated without being ready to fight, Germany would declare war at once. Nothing but the spectacle of the strong man armed and standing on the threshold could scare off the burglar who was threatening the House of Peace.

When Russia had let pass the time limit set by Germany, when France had answered that she would act according to her own interests, then the German Empire had to mobilize its army and go ahead. Before one German soldier had crossed the German frontier, a large number of aëroplanes came flying into our country across the neutral territory of Belgium and Luxemburg, without a word of warning on the part of the Belgian Government. At the same time the German Government learned that the French were about to enter Belgium.

"Truth about Germany" sounds the top-note of hypocrisy with these words: "When Russia had let pass the time limit set by Germany, when France had answered that she would act according to her own interests, then the German Empire had to mobilize its army and go ahead." (Why should Germany go ahead with Austria's quarrel after Austria herself had come to an agreement with Russia? Of course, it is patent that Ger-

many feared, after all, her efforts, there WOULD
BE NO WAR.) What did the bully expect?
He had issued an impudent ultimatum to the
masters of twelve millions of soldiers, irresistibly
recalling the story of Canute when he had his
throne set below high-water mark as the tide was
coming in. It sounds like a piece of ill-timed
humor that aëroplanes after this flew across neutral territory without a word of warning on the
part of the Belgian Government. The Belgian
Government may not have been looking out of
their bedroom windows.

The best reply to all this talk of Belgian neutrality having been infringed by France and
Belgium is that it was never suggested at the time
when Great Britain asked Germany her intentions
about Belgium; and it would have made a very
plausible reply. But it clearly had not even been
invented then, and is an afterthought " ad hoc "
for American consumption. France had not
received the necessary invitation from Belgium
to send her troops till August 5th or 6th. The
French Ambassador in England had it telegraphed
to him on August 6th. German troops had
already entered Belgium on August 4th.

Then our Government with great reluctance
had to decide upon requesting the Belgian Government to allow our troops to march through its
territory. Belgium was to be indemnified after
the war, was to retain its sovereignty and integrity.
Belgium protested, at the same time allowing,
by an agreement with France, that the French

troops might enter Belgium. After all this and not till France and Belgium itself had broken the neutrality, our troops entered the neutral territory. Germany wanted nothing from Belgium, but had to prevent that Belgian soil be used as a gate of entrance into German territory.

To say that " at the same time the German Government learned that the French were about to enter Belgium" is another of the most colossal misstatements of a book which handles the truth very carelessly. The British Government, still in doubt as to whether it should enter the arena, on July 31st demanded categorical assurances from the French and German Governments that they would respect the neutrality of Belgium. The French Government, without any reserve and with obvious sincerity, replied in the affirmative at once. The German Secretary of State said that he must consult the Emperor and the Chancellor before he could possibly answer. His insincerity was obvious. The Kaiser and the Chancellor did not answer, and the British Ambassador delivered his ultimatum on August 4th.

There was this awkwardness about their answering Great Britain—that they were requesting, or had made up their minds to request, the Belgian Government to allow German troops to march through its territory. Belgium was to be indemnified after the war, to retain its sovereignty and integrity and all the rest of it. Belgium refused point-blank, and said that it would defend its rights as a sovereign power with all

4

its forces. "Truth about Germany" was not "Truth about Belgium," for it says: "Not till France and Belgium itself had broken the neutrality, did German troops enter Belgium." This is an absolute lie, about on a par with a statement in the next sentence: "Germany wanted nothing from Belgium, but had to prevent that Belgian soil be used as a gate of entrance into German territory."

There is abundant evidence to prove that Germany had arranged to invade France through Belgian territory. Bernhardi and other German military writers have always told us this plan would be pursued, and we have good reason to know the soundness of Bernhardi's forecasts! In the middle of July a warning came to Americans in Brussels from San Francisco, telling them to get out of Belgium by the end of the month, if they wanted to get out at all.

Little has as yet been said of Great Britain. It was Germany's conviction that the sincerity of Britain's love for peace could be trusted. At any rate Sir Edward Grey and Mr. Asquith asserted again and again in the course of the last few years that England wished friendly relations with Germany and never would lend its support to a Franco-Russian attack on Germany. Now this attack had been made; Germany was on the defensive against two powerful enemies. What would Great Britain do about it? That was the question.

The most naïve confession in the whole book is: "It was Germany's conviction that the sincerity of Great Britain's love for peace could be trusted." Can anyone doubt that British blindness and folly were reckoned as an asset to Germany when the Kaiser determined on the war. England to Germany was Ethelred the Unready. That was the chief of the diplomatic blunders of the man upon whom the mantle of Bismarck had fallen. We will allow that the British Prime Minister and Foreign Minister promised the German Ambassador every time he asked them that England would never lend its support to a Franco-Russian attack on Germany. But we can be much more certain of the reply which the German Ambassador would have received if he had asked would Great Britain tolerate Germany's picking a quarrel with France and Russia to inaugurate a war of conquest, which was, in effect, asking Great Britain to wait for her turn until her Allies were overwhelmed.

Great Britain asked in return for its neutrality that the German forces should not enter Belgium. In other words, it asked that Germany should allow the French and Belgian troops to form on Belgian territory for a march against our frontier! This we could not allow. It would have been suicidal.

It was in this context that Chancellor von Bethmann-Hollweg immortalized himself with his phrase, "a scrap of paper." That, he gave the world to understand, was the German definition of a treaty. When Great Britain, as the price of her neutrality, demanded that Germany should respect the integrity of Belgium, which she, equally with Great Britain, had guaranteed, the candid German inquired if Great Britain was going to war for a " scrap of paper "! Great Britain announced that she would go to war if Germany did not make up her mind to respect that scrap of paper before midnight. And the United States made a note of the phrase to guide it in its future diplomatic negotiations with Germany. It was in vain that Germany protested that its neutrality would allow the French and Belgian troops to form on Belgian territory for a march against the German frontier. The whole thing is a lie, but the phrase " and Belgian troops," contains an insult too—to suggest that Belgium meant to attack Germany is a piece of colossal impertinence. Unfortunately for Germany, Great Britain had addressed a similar note to France, and France had undertaken categorically not to enter Belgium unless Germany entered it first. It was not until at least a day after German troops had invaded Belgium that France received any invitation to send troops into Belgium.

The German Government made Great Britain in return for its neutrality the following offers: We would not attack the northern coast of France, we would leave unmolested the maritime commerce of France and would indemnify Belgium after the war and safeguard its sovereignty and integrity.

But Germany greatly desired the neutrality of Great Britain, for with Britain at war with her, her fleet and her commerce would be confined to a handful of fifth-rate ports in the Baltic, so she offered in return for British neutrality to leave the northern coast of France unmolested, not to take any territory from France except her colonies, and to indemnify Belgium and safeguard its sovereignty and integrity when the war was over. To this Mr. Asquith made his famous reply in the House of Commons on August 6th:

"INFAMOUS PROPOSALS.

"What did that proposal amount to? In the first place, it meant this: that behind the back of France, which was not to be made a party to these communications at all, we should have given, if we had assented to them, free license to Germany to annex in the event of a successful war the whole of the extra-European dominions and possessions of France. What did it mean as regards Belgium? If Belgium, when she addressed, as she did address in these last days, her moving appeal to us to fulfil our solemn guarantee of her neutrality, what reply should we have given? What reply could we have given to that Belgian appeal? We should have been obliged to say that without her knowledge we had bartered away to the Power that was threatening her our obligations to keep our plighted word. (Loud and prolonged cheers.)

"Sir, the House has read, and the country has read, in the course of the last few hours the most pathetic address by the King of the Belgians to his people. (Cheers.) I do not envy the man who could read that appeal with unmoved heart. (Cheers.) The Belgians are fighting, they are losing their lives. (Loud cheers.) What would have been the position of Great Britain to-day in the face of that spectacle if we had assented to this infamous proposal? (Loud and prolonged cheers.)

"Yes, and what were we to get in return? For the

betrayal of our friends and the dishonor of our obligations, what were we to get in return? We were to get a promise— nothing more (laughter)—as to what Germany would do in certain eventualities, a promise, be it observed—I am sorry to have to say it, but it must be put upon record—a promise given by a Power which was at that very moment announcing its intention to violate its own Treaty obligations (cheers), and inviting us to do the same. I can only say, if we had even dallied or temporized with such an offer, we, as a Government, should have covered ourselves with dishonor. We should have betrayed the interests of this country of which we are the trustees. (Cheers.)

"I am glad to turn to the reply which my right honorable friend (Sir Edward Grey) made, and from which I will read to the House one or two of the more salient passages, because this document, No. 101, puts on record a week ago the attitude of the British Government, and, as I believe, of the British people. My right honorable friend says: 'His Majesty's Government cannot for a moment entertain the Chancellor's proposal that they should bind themselves to neutrality on such terms. What he asks us is in effect to engage to stand by while French colonies are taken and France is beaten so long as Germany does not take French territory as distinct from the colonies. From the material point of view'—my right honorable friend (Sir Edward Grey) uses, as he always does, very temperate language—'such a proposal is unacceptable; for France, without further territory in Europe being taken from her, could be so crushed as to lose her position as a Great Power and become subordinate to German policy.'

"That is the material aspect. He proceeds: 'Altogether apart from that it would be a disgrace to us to make this bargain with Germany at the expense of France, a disgrace from which the good name of this country would never recover. (Loud cheers.) The Chancellor also in effect asks us to bargain away whatever obligations or interests we have as regards the neutrality of Belgium. We could not entertain that bargain either.'"

In spite of this Great Britain declared war on

Germany and sides to-day with those Continental Powers that have united for our destruction, in order that Muscovite barbarism may rule Europe. We know that Germany did not deserve such treatment on the part of Great Britain, and do not believe that Great Britain by this action did a service to humanity and civilization.

> Great Britain did not join in the war in order that Muscovite barbarism might rule Europe, but to rid Europe's long-suffering civilization from German militarism which sat on its neck and was choking it, like the Old Man of the Sea in the story of " Sindbad the Sailor."
>
> Probably not even Austria, which did not declare war on Great Britain for a good many days afterwards, would dispute that Germany richly deserved this treatment from Great Britain. The United States, which, as this book observes, is the only great neutral Power, has preached from nearly every platform, pulpit, and newspaper office on the North American continent, that Great Britain, like the Good Samaritan, came to the rescue of Humanity and Civilization instead of standing by on the other side of the road while thieves massacred their victims.

To-day we are facing hard facts. Germany has to fight for her existence. She will fight knowing that the great Powers beyond the ocean will do her justice as soon as they know the truth.

> What Germany may expect from the United States is the Judgment of Solomon.

FOREWORD TO CHAPTER III

Letter in *The Times*, September 22nd, 1914:

"RUSSIA *v.* PRUSSIA.

"But what are such facts as these to the profound intuitions of Mr. Keir Hardie and Mr. Ramsay MacDonald? On the other hand, they deplore our conflict with the cultivated and amiable Prussian Empire. Its huge fleet, its inexhaustible store of submarine mines, its carefully concealed preparation of hundreds of bomb-dropping aëroplanes and Zeppelins, its great system of strategic railways upon the Belgian and Polish frontiers, its secret manufacture of vast siege-guns, its incessant increases of its stupendous army, its leap—prepared and armed—into this war, they regard as evidence of an excessive anxiety to keep the peace. Had we but let Germany 'finish' Belgium and France, and reduce Russia to the present position of Austria in a Three-Emperor League, then the peace of the world, the security of Britain, the welfare of our millions of workers would have been assured for ever. We might then have given up building more warships, confident in the Kaiser's secured good-will. But for the wickedness of Sir Edward Grey.

"We protest against this insult to the intelligence and self-respect of our fellow Britons which Mr. Hardie and Mr. MacDonald are offering, and we protest still more strongly against the stupid, ignorant, mischievous misrepresentation of a great, kindly, friendly people upon which their case is based.

"C. HAGBERG WRIGHT.
"H. G. WELLS."

From *The Times*, August 6th, 1914.

"New York, August 4th.

". . . The American Press holds that the German Emperor has proved himself the enemy of civilization, and it does not hesitate to say so in the strongest terms it can command.   The *Chicago Tribune* decorates its article on the Kaiser's invocation of Divine assistance with the single word 'Blasphemy.'   The *New York Times* gives its complete editorial endorsement to the words of the Paris *Temps* that Russians, Frenchmen, and Englishmen must stand united against 'the powers of brigandage.'   In this war, says the *New York World*, Germany and Austria have no sympathizers even among the neutrals.   It continues:

"'The enlightened opinion of the whole world has turned against the two Kaisers as it turned against Napoleon when he sought to make himself autocrat of Europe.   German autocracy is isolated, but what was begun as a war of autocracy is not unlikely to end as a war of revolution, with thrones crumbling and dynasties ending in exile.   Civilization cannot rest at the mercy of despotism, and the welfare of mankind is not to be made the plaything of autocracy.   In the vanguard of the twentieth century in most respects, Germany has straggled back to the seventeenth century politically.   The curse of mediæval government has hung over her noblest achievements.   Every impulse toward political freedom has been beaten back by the Mailed Fist.   Austria's quarrel with Servia was no affair of the German people.   Russia's challenge to Austria was no affair of the German people.   Yet the very fate of the German Empire is thrown into the balance in order to halt the march of political freedom in Europe.   Germany desires to crush, not Russian despotism, but French Republicanism.   Britain is compelled to make France's cause her cause.'"

From *The Times*, August 29th, 1914.

"Toronto, August 27th.

"According to Colonel Hughes, Minister of Militia, sixty thousand citizens of the United States have offered to enlist in the Canadian Expeditionary Forces.   These expressed the simple desire to fight for the British Empire.   Application was even made in person to the Militia Department at Ottawa.   Of course, no Americans could be enrolled."

CHAPTER III

ENGLAND, FRANCE, AND RUSSIA, UNTHREATENED
BY GERMANY, GO TO WAR FOR POLITICAL
REASONS—GERMANY DEFENDS HER INDEPEND-
ENCE AND FIGHTS FOR HER VERY EXISTENCE,
FOR HER FUTURE AS A GREAT POWER—HOW
A PEACEFUL PEOPLE WERE IMBUED WITH THE
SPIRIT OF WAR.

IT may be well to quote the terms in which
France and Russia were unthreatened by
Germany. They are confessed by the writers of
this book only two or three pages back in these
words: "When Russia had let pass the time
limit set by Germany, when France had answered
that she would act according to her own interests." The German White Paper on the war
with Russia uses these words: "The Imperial
Ambassador at St. Petersburg was ordered on the
afternoon of July 31st to advise the Russian
Government that Germany had declared a state
of war as a countermove to the mobilization of the
Russian army and navy, which would have to be
followed by mobilization unless Russia ceased her
military preparations against Germany and Aus-

58

tria-Hungary within twelve hours, and so advised
Germany. At the same time, the Imperial
Ambassador at Paris was directed to request an
explanation from the French Government within
eighteen hours as to whether, in the case of a
Russo-German war, France would remain neutral."

When did an ultimatum cease to be a threat?
But instead of threatening Great Britain, Germany tried to cheat her. The result is that
Germany, as the book says, is fighting for her
very existence. And so are we.

The last days of the month of July were days
of anxiety and distress for the German people.
They hoped that they would be permitted to
preserve an honorable peace. A few months
earlier, in 1913, when the centennial of the war
for independence from French oppression and the
twenty-fifth anniversary of Emperor William's
ascent of the throne had been celebrated, they
had willingly taken upon their shoulders the great
sacrifice of the so-called "Wehrvorlage," which
increased the peace strength of the standing army
enormously and cost one billion marks. They
considered it simply as an increase of these peace
insurance premiums.

All reasonable people are prepared to admit
that the German people, as distinct from the
projectors of the present campaign and the cour-
tiers of the German Canute, sincerely hoped
that they would be "permitted to preserve an

honorable peace." And in so doing, they deserve the sympathy of the world. But they must
have had a genius for self-deception if they
considered the enormous additions to the army
and the war levy of fifty millions as "an insurance premium for peace." It was like giving a
boy a new gun and a hundred cartridges, and
telling him on no account to put the cartridges
into the gun.

Our diplomats worked hard for the maintenance
of peace, for the localization of the Austro-Servian
war. So sure were the leading men of the Empire
of the preservation of general peace that at the
beginning of the week which was to bring general
mobilization they said to each other joyfully:
"Next week our vacation time begins." But
they were fearfully disappointed. Russia's unex-
pected, treacherous mobilization compelled Germany to draw the sword also. On the evening of
the first day of August the one word, Mobilization! was flashed by the electric spark all over
the country. There was no more anxiety and
uncertainty. Cool, firm resolution at once per-
meated the entire German folk. The Reichstag
was called together for an extra session.

The German method of diplomacy for the
localization of the Austro-Servian war was a coup
like the 1909 coup for the localization of Bosnia
and Herzegovina in the Austrian Empire. The
bully had threatened again to knock Russia down
if she interfered. If the leading men of the Ger-

man Empire were so sure of the preservation of
general peace, it was because they believed that
Russia would once more funk a fight. But as the
book says: "They were fearfully disappointed."
They call Russia's refusal to be bullied an "un-
expected, treacherous mobilization." There was
nothing for Germany to do but to fulfill her threat.

It must be confessed that when Germany found
that her challenge to fight was unexpectedly
accepted, she behaved with the courage and
dignity of a nation of warriors.

Three days later, on the anniversary of the
battles of Weissenburg and Spicheren, the representatives of the German people met. This
session, which lasted only a few hours, proved
worthy of the great historical moment marking
the beginning of such a conflagration as the world
had never seen before. The railroad lines were
under military control and used almost exclusively
for purposes of mobilization. In spite of all such
difficulties, more than 300 to the 397 deputies
managed to get to Berlin in time. The rest sent
word that they were unable to come. On the
evening of August 3d the Imperial Chancellor
called the leaders of all parties, including the
Socialists, to his house and explained to them in
a concise and impressive statement how frivolously
Germany had been driven to war.

If the German Chancellor was able to make "a
concise and impressive statement," showing

"how frivolously Germany had been driven to war," it was a masterpiece of hypocrisy. For, at such a crisis, the Emperor must have trusted him to a certain extent, and he was therefore in all probability pretty fully aware of all the ingenious traps laid for England, France, and Russia. He must have known of the studied precautions which were taken to prevent Servia by any possibility acceding to the Austrian demand: he must have known how the Emperor plotted to ensure Russia's either accepting the humiliation of allowing Servia to be crushed, or being compelled to fight: he must have known of all the ingenious expedients, especially the German Ambassador's continued residence in Paris long after the war had broken out, in order to lull the French into delaying their military preparations: he must have known all the Jesuitical reservations made in the pourparlers between Germany and England in order, if possible, to keep England neutral.

With all this private information in his head he had to maintain to the Reichstag that Germany had been "driven frivolously to war," and if he did it concisely and impressively, he must be a master of speaking with his tongue in his cheek.

But I suspect that the guileless writer of this book has done him an injustice.

At the time of this meeting the unanimous acceptance of all war measures by the Reichstag was already assured. In numerous conferences the heads of the several departments explained the contents and meaning of the bills to be sub-

mitted to the Reichstag. The participants of
the conferences showed already what spirit would
characterize the next day. The session of the
Reichstag filled the entire German nation with
pride and enthusiasm; the Reichstag maintained
the dignity of the German Empire and the German
people.

In greater numbers than ever before, the deputies, high officers of the army and navy and the
civil government assembled on August 4th, first
in houses of worship to pray to God, and then in
the royal castle of Berlin. The military character
of the ceremony at the opening of the session
showed under what auspices this memorable act
took place.

**We may be sure that this meeting of the great-
est men in Germany on such an historic occasion
was impressive and dignified in the highest
degree.**

The Kaiser entered the hall in the simple gray
field uniform, without the usual pomp, accompanied by chamberlains and court officials and
pages in glittering court dresses. Only state
ministers, generals, and admirals followed him to
the throne, from where he read his speech, after
covering his head with his helmet. His voice
betrayed the strain under which he was laboring.
Repeatedly he was interrupted by enthusiastic
applause, and when he closed, a rousing cheer
thundered through the famous White Hall, some-

thing that had never before occurred since the
erection of the old castle. Then came a surprise.
The Emperor laid down the manuscript of his
speech and continued speaking. From now on
he knew only Germans, he said, no differences of
party, creed, religion, or social position, and he
requested the party leaders to give him their
hands as a pledge that they all would stand by
him "in Not und Tod"—in death and distress.
This scene was entirely impromptu, and thus so
much more impressive and touching.

> The Kaiser has, one is sure, suffered from his
> chroniclers, for the German lacks the saving
> sense of humor which is demanded in the British
> or American journalist, and has made his sover-
> eign appear with the adjuncts of the principal
> tenor in an opera and innumerable stage direc-
> tions. I am sure that William II. was in reality
> manly, dignified, and heroic in the highest degree,
> but your German journalist is as crude in his
> methods as the monkish chroniclers of the Middle
> Ages.
> The Kaiser may be theatrical by disposition,
> but on such an occasion, when the moment had
> at last arrived, his exaltation would have him
> feel like a genuine Nibelung.

And it was hardly over, when the Reichstag
—an unheard of proceeding in such surroundings
—began to sing the German national hymn:
"Heil Dir im Siegerkranz." The magnificent
hall, until then only the scene of pompous court

festivities, witnessed an outburst of patriotism
such as had never been seen there before. To
the accompaniment of loud cheers, the Kaiser
walked out, after shaking the hands of the Imperial
Chancellor and the chief of the General Staff,
von Moltke.

One hour later the Reichstag met in its own
house. The Emperor had begged for quick and
thorough work. He was not to be disappointed.
Without any formalities the presiding officers of
the last session were re-elected—in times of peace
and party strife, this would have been impossible.
This short curtain-raiser being over, the first act
of the drama began. Before an overcrowded
house, the Chancellor described simply and
clearly the efforts of the Government for the preservation of peace. He stated cold facts, showing
unmistakably Russia's double dealing and justi-
fying Germany's beginning of a war which she
did not want. The Chancellor had begun in a
quiet, subdued tone. Then he raised his voice,
and when, in words that rang through the hall,
he declared that the entire nation was united the
deputies and the spectators in the galleries could
sit still no longer. They rose, with them at first
some Socialists, then all of them carried away by
the impulse of the moment; the members of the
Federal Council, of the Press, Diplomats, and the
crowds in the galleries joined them. The whole
multitude cheered and clapped its hands franti-
cally. It reflected truly the spirit of the whole

5

nation. The Speaker who, under ordinary circumstances, would have suppressed the clapping
of hands as unparliamentary and the demonstra-
tions of the galleries as undignified, let the patriotic
outburst go on to its end.

**When the Reichstag met in its own house, it
did its work with soldierly brevity, though the
Chancellor was compelled once more to describe
the duplicity of Germany and ascribe it all to
Russia. It was of no consequence; everyone
believed him implicitly, and everyone present
went mad with joy and patriotism.**

After a short intermission the business meeting
began. Sixteen war measures had been introduced,
the most important of which was the one asking
for five billion marks to carry on the war. The
leader of the Social Democrats read a statement
explaining why his party, despite its opposition
on principle to all Army and Navy appropriations,
would vote for the proposed bills. Without
further debates all the bills were passed, and
shortly after 5 P.M. the Reichstag adjourned.
At 7 P.M. the Emperor received the presiding
officers of the Reichstag to thank them for their
prompt and useful work. He signed the bills,
which were immediately published and thus became laws.

**A war credit of two hundred and fifty millions
was voted without any man in the room knowing
exactly how it was going to be raised.**

The resolute attitude and quick work of the
Reichstag reflected the unity and resolution of
the entire nation. Sixty-seven millions of Germans feel, think, and act with their elected representatives. No party, no class, no creed is
standing back; all are imbued with one single
thought: United Germany is unconquerable.

**Obviously no party, no class, no creed was
standing back. Everyone present believed implicitly that united Germany was unconquerable.**

The entire German people *are* united as never
before in their history. Even one hundred and
one years ago, in 1813, the entire population cannot
have been so uniformly seized by the spirit of
war as at the outbreak of this struggle, which is
the people's war in the truest sense of the word,
and which was predicted by Bismarck. All
reigning princes are going out to fight with the
army, and have appointed their wives as regents.
Instances include the Kaiser's son-in-law, the
Duke of Brunswick, who appointed his consort,
the only daughter of the Emperor, as Regent.
The princes call their people to arms, and they
themselves stand ready to sacrifice all they have.

**We are told that the German people is united
as it never has been before. If this is true it is
because they are conscious that the struggle is
one of life and death. But if this is the people's
war, as the writers of this book maintain, it shows**

(which every humane person must be unwilling to believe) that the German people shares the Emperor's blind lust of power and is willing to submit to the most tyrannical militarism in order that there may be a German hegemony of Europe —a German Empire as absolute as that which groaned under the Roman Nero. Bismarck is said to have predicted that this would be a people's war. I cannot help thinking that Bismarck would have had some very acid things to say about this war, and especially about the diplomatic efforts of the Wilhelmstrasse which had preceded it.

This example from above carried the nation with them. The Reichstag knew parties and factions no more, and neither does the nation. The Emperor sounded the word which has become common property from Königsberg to Constance, from Upper Silesia to the Belgian frontier: "I know only Germans!" And yet how terribly is our nation disrupted by party strife. Ill-advised persons across our frontiers hoped that creed differences would make for disunion; Frenchmen and Russians expected to weaken our Empire with the aid of Alsatians and Poles. This hope has been destroyed—we are a united people, as united as was the Reichstag, the Socialists included. The latter have for years voted against all Army and Navy appropriations, have advocated international peace, and last year voted against the bills increasing the Army strength.

In many foreign quarters strong hopes were nourished that this party would help them. But those men did not know our German people. Our civilization, our independence as a nation, was threatened, and in that moment party interest or creed existed no more. The true German heart is beating only for the Fatherland; east and west, north and south, Protestants, Catholics, and Jews, are "a united people of brethren in the hour of danger." When Germany was so threatened by Russia, when the German "Peace Emperor" was shamefully betrayed by the Czar of all the Russians, then there was but one sacred party in existence—the party of Germans.

No rumors have reached us to disprove the claim of the writers that all Germans, even Alsatians and Poles, are unanimous in their patriotism at the present moment, though the Poles may show their hand and be just as rapturous about Russia when the Russian armies enter Posen, for they have always been unconquerably hostile to Germanization in any form. It remains to be seen how the one sacred party in existence, the party of the Germans, will survive the Russian conquest of Prussian Poland.

FOREWORD TO CHAPTER IV

Letter from Mr. H. M. Hyndman, protesting against branding all Germans with the desire for war, in *The Times*, August 18th, 1914.

"'The demonstration against war in Berlin only the other day, in spite of the attacks of the police and the soldiery, was the most imposing ever held in that great city. From the very first the German Social Democratic Party, which polled no fewer than 4,250,000 votes at the last General Election, those being votes of men over twenty-five years of age; which receives weekly subscriptions from more than 1,000,000 persons; which has close upon 100 daily newspapers belonging to and issued by the party; and which is estimated to form one-third of the German Army—from the very first, I say, this great body of working people has vehemently denounced the war. It has continued to do so in the face of bitter persecution, and, as is reported, of the imprisonment and execution of some of its noblest leaders. Quite recently, not more than three days ago, its managers contrived to issue a stirring manifesto in favor of peace, though the journals of the party have been suppressed and the printing presses closed.'"

The Times, August 25th, 1914.

"All have been struck by the wonderful readiness of Germany—striking evidence, if more were needed, of her long secret preparations for war while she still pretended to seek peace; and they are thus able to discount, from their own experience, the allegation which has been sedulously circulated among the American visitors to the effect that war has been thrust upon an unwilling and unexpecting Germany by neighbors jealous of her commercial success.

"At Munich in particular, the scene appears to have been a very striking one. The park in Luisenstrasse was closed to the public, and for two whole days a stream of artisans and peasants, many in the picturesque costume of the Tyrol, passed in at one of the gates, emerging at the other end as smart soldiers, fully armed and equipped. Everywhere entirely new outfits, complete to the last button, have apparently been issued to officers and men alike, to dazzle the eyes of the ladies of Paris. The men were carefully divided into groups according to height and marched off to the spot where uniforms to fit them were waiting."

CHAPTER IV

THE GERMAN MOBILIZATION

THE CLOCKWORK OF MOBILIZATION; PERFECT OR-
DER AND QUIET EVERYWHERE—GENERAL
ACCEPTANCE BY ALL CLASSES AND FACTIONS
OF THE NECESSITIES OF A WAR NOT SOUGHT
BY GERMANY.

THE German mobilization was the greatest
movement of people that the world has ever
seen. Nearly four million men had to be transported from every part of the empire to her borders. The manner in which this population is
distributed made this task extremely difficult.
Berlin, Rhenish-Westphalia, Upper Silesia, and
Saxony especially had to send their contingents
in every direction, since the eastern provinces are
more thinly settled and had to have a stronger
guard for the borders immediately. The result
was a hurrying to and fro of thousands and hundreds of thousands of soldiers, besides a flood of
civilians who had to reach their homes as soon as
possible. Countries where the population is more
regularly distributed have an easier task than
Germany, with its predominating urban popula-

tion.   The difficulties of the gigantic undertaking
were also increased by the necessity for transport-
ing war materials of every sort.   In the west are
chiefly industrial undertakings, in the east mainly
agricultural. Horse-raising is mostly confined to
the provinces on the North Sea and the Baltic,
but chiefly to East Prussia, and this province, the
farthest away from France, had to send its best
horses to the western border, as did also Schleswig-
Holstein and Hanover.   Coal for our warships
had to go in the other direction.   From the Rhen-
ish mines it went to the North Sea, from Upper
Silesia to the Baltic.   Ammunition and heavy
projectiles were transported from the central part
of the empire to the borders.   And everywhere
these operations had to be carried on with haste.
One can thus say that the German mobilization
was the greatest movement of men and materials
that the world has ever seen.

> **The clockwork mobilization described goes far
> to prove that if the war was not sought by Ger-
> many, Germany was perfectly certain that the
> path it was pursuing might bring it to war at
> any moment.   It was a marvel of efficiency and
> organization.**

And how was it carried on?   No one could have
wondered if there had been hundreds of unforeseen
incidents, if military trains had arrived at their
stations with great delays, if there had resulted
in many places a wild hugger-mugger from the

tremendous problems on hand. But there was
not a trace of this. On the Monday evening of
the first week of mobilization a high officer of the
General Staff said: "It had to go well to-day,
but how about to-morrow, the main day?"
Tuesday evening saw no reason for complaint,
no delay, no requests for instructions. All had
moved with the regularity of clockwork. Regiments that had been ordered to mobilize in the
forenoon left in the evening for the field, fully
equipped. Not a man was lacking. There were
no deserters, no shirkers, no cowards. Instead,
there were volunteers whose numbers far exceeded
the number that could be used. Every German
wanted to do his duty.

> **It helps a man to do his duty, if he knows that
> he will be shot if he fails to do it, and that he is
> registered at the local police-station like a
> "Ticket-of-Leave" man.**

The most noteworthy thing was the earnest
quietness with which the gigantic gathering proceeded. Not a city, not a village reported unrest
or even an untoward incident. The separation
was hard for many a soldier. Many a volunteer
tore himself away from his dear ones with bleeding
heart, but with face beaming with the light of
one who looks forward to victory. Following the
Kaiser's wish, those who remained behind filled the
churches, and, kneeling, prayed to God for victory for the just German cause. The folk-war,
brought on by the wantonness of the opponents,

in itself brought peace and order, safety and discipline.   Never, probably, have the police had
fewer excesses to deal with than in the days of
the mobilization, although great crowds gathered
constantly in every city.

> This " folk-war, brought on by the wantonness
> of opponents," was remarkable for the orderli-
> ness of its mobilization.
> This is indeed wonderful! The sixty-seven
> millions of the population of Germany, unless they
> are belied by the authors of this book, persuaded
> themselves that it was worth while to be immedi-
> ately shut out from the sea, on which they had
> built up such an enormous commerce, and to run
> the more than probable risk of losing their
> commerce altogether, and all their Colonial
> possessions, and their Navy, and their place in
> the world, in order that Russia might be humili-
> ated and Austria allowed to crush Servia (which,
> though they did not know it, might be more than
> Austria could accomplish).   More ardent stu-
> dents of politics, more ardent devotees of the aim
> that the German Emperor should be the successor
> not only of the Holy Roman Emperors, but of the
> Roman Emperors themselves, might grimly re-
> joice that the day had arrived for Germany to
> throw down her gauntlet and make good her claim
> to be mistress of the world.   But I think that
> they were comparatively few—that the humilia-
> tion of Russia and the chastisement of Servia
> were " bonnes bouches " sufficient for the self-
> satisfaction of the ordinary Sausage-machine.

The best criterion of the enthusiasm of the
people is without doubt the number of volunteers.
More than one million of these, a number greater
than that of the standing army, presented themselves within a few days. There were sons of the
nobility, university students, farmers, merchants,
common laborers. No calling hung back. Every
young man sorrowed when he was rejected. No
section of the Fatherland was unrepresented, not
even the Reichsland Alsace-Lorraine, where, indeed, the number of volunteers was conspicuously
great. When the lists in various cities had to be
closed, the young men who had not been accepted
turned away with tears in their eyes, and telegraphed from regiment to regiment, hoping to
find one where there were still vacancies. Where
the sons of the wealthy renounced the pleasures
of youth and the comforts of their homes to accept
the hardships of war in serving the Fatherland,
the poor and the poorest appeared in like degree.
In families having four or five sons subject to
military duty, a youngest son, not yet liable for
service, volunteered. The year 1870, truly a
proud year 1870, saw nothing like this.

> At all events, according to the authors of this
> book, the war was received with universal en-
> thusiasm. " More than a million volunteers
> came forward within a few days." I am afraid
> that this statement sounds suspicious. I cannot
> believe that the German military authorities,
> when there was any chance of their entering upon

the greatest war in history, would be likely to
leave out of the various classes available for service more than a million men of fighting age. If
the writers include in this number the educated
men who had done their year's voluntary service
and were merely anticipating the period at which
they would be called to the colors, they would not
be called volunteers in England; they would be
reservists. It is calculated that the only sons and
others not liable to military service at all, who
volunteered and were accepted, were under
50,000. I am not detracting from the merit of the
patriots who would not wait till their turn came to
be called up, but clamored to be taken at once.
All patriots are splendid, and Germany is richer
in patriots than almost any other country. I am
only taking exception to the word " volunteers,"
which is not used in the sense in which we should
use it, and which has probably been advisedly
used by the translator to influence American
opinion. This is not needed in the case of Germans, whose military ardor is a proverb.

A thing that raised the national enthusiasm still
higher was the appearance of the troops in brand-
new uniforms, complete from head to foot. The
first sight of these new uniforms, of modest field-
gray, faultlessly made, evoked everywhere the
question: Where did they come from? On the
first day of mobilization dozens of cloth manufacturers appeared at the war ministry with offers
of the new material. "We don't need any," was
the astonishing reply. Equal amazement was

caused by the faultless new boots and shoes of
the troops, especially in view of the recent famous
"boot speech" of the French Senator Humbert.

Small arms, cannons, and ammunitions are so
plentiful that they have merely to be unpacked.
In view of all this, it is no wonder that the regiments marching in were everywhere greeted with
jubilation, and that those marching out took leave
of their garrisons with joyful songs.   No one thinks
of death and destruction, every one of victory
and a happy reunion. German discipline, once
so slandered, now celebrates its triumph.

> The fatuousness of the writer or writers of this
> book is nowhere more hopelessly in evidence than
> in this paragraph. " A thing that raised the
> national enthusiasm still higher " (than the glory
> of Germany and her fight for existence) " was
> the appearance of the troops in brand-new uni-
> forms complete from head to foot. The first sight
> of these new uniforms of modest field-gray,
> faultlessly made, etc. . . . Equal amazement
> was caused by the faultless new boots and shoes
> of the troops, etc."
>
> Two reflections are provoked by these banali-
> ties. The first is: Could anything be more
> trivial in this crisis of their national existence?
> And the second is: How could they have had
> fresh uniforms ready for four million troops if
> war was not expected?
>
> Of course war was expected, for " small arms,
> cannons, and ammunitions " were so plentiful
> that they merely had to be unpacked, and so

much had been said about what they were going
to do that the troops were convinced of easy
victory, and went away singing, which led the
egregious writer of this book to remark: " German discipline, once so slandered, now celebrates
its triumph "—"a non sequitur," as it appears to
me.

There was still another matter in which the
troops gave their countrymen cause for rejoicing.
Not one drunken man was seen during these
earnest days in the city streets. The General
Staff had, moreover, wisely ordered that during
the mobilization, when everyone had money in
his pockets, alcoholic drinks were not to be sold
at the railroad stations. Despite this, the soldiers
did not lack for refreshments on their journey.
Women and girls offered their services to the Red
Cross, and there was no station where coffee, tea,
milk, and substantial food were not at the disposal
of the soldiers. They were not required to suffer
hunger or any other discomfort. The German
anti-alcoholists are rejoicing at this earnest tribute
to their principles, which were at first laughed at,
and then pitied, but triumphed in the days of the
mobilization.

It was humorous of the writer to remark in one
sentence that the troops rejoiced their countrymen because not one drunken man was seen in
those days, and in the next sentence to mention
that the drink-shops were shut. But one ap-

plauds the taking of these measures for sobriety in Germany as they have been taken in England and Russia. The elevation of the soldier is a matter of first-class importance, but he had better by far be drunk than murder Red Cross nurses or drive women and children in front of a column when it is exposed to the machine-guns of the enemy. It is pleasant to record that the troops were everywhere offered tea and coffee.

The army is increased to many times its ordinary strength by the mobilization. It draws from everywhere millions of soldiers, workmen, horses, wagons, and other material. The entire railway service is at its disposal. The mobilization of the fleet goes on more quietly and less conspicuously, but not less orderly and smoothly. Indeed, it is, even in peace times, practically mobilized as to its greatest and strongest units. For this reason its transports are smaller than those of the army; they are concentrated in a few harbors, and therefore do not attract so much public attention. The naval transports, working in accordance to plans in connection with those of the army, have moved their quotas of men and materials with the most punctual exactitude. The naval reserve of fully-trained officers and men is practically inexhaustible. The faithful work of our shipbuilding concerns, carried on uninterruptedly day and night under plans carefully prepared in time of peace, has wrought for our navy a strong increase in powerful warships.

I am afraid that the writer of this egregious book cannot be trusted as to military details. He says: " The army is increased to many times its ordinary strength by mobilization." Say for the sake of argument that the German army consists of a million men on a peace footing, does our author mean that after mobilization it was increased to twenty or forty millions? Indeed, these figures do not seem to be large enough for him, since he says in the next sentence: " It draws FROM EVERYWHERE MILLIONS of soldiers, workmen, horses, wagons, and other material." At this rate it seems safer to put the strength of the army down at a billion; he is very fond of billions. And what does he mean when he says that the mobilization of the fleet goes on "more quietly but not less orderly and smoothly"? And what does he mean by saying that the naval transports are smaller than those of the army? or "the faithful work of our shipbuilding concerns carried on uninterruptedly day and night under plans carefully prepared in time of peace has wrought for our navy a strong increase in powerful warships"? Does he mean by this that the German dockyards have been working day and night because they knew that war was certain in August, 1914, or does he mean nothing at all in particular?

As is known, the German fleet is built on the so-called "assumption-of-risk" plan. That is, it is intended that it shall be so strong that even the strongest sea-power, in a conflict with the

Germans, risks forfeiting its former rôle as a world factor. This "risk" idea has been hammered into the heart of every German seaman, and they are all eager to win for the fleet such glory that it can be favorably contrasted with the deeds of the old and the new armies.

We know that the German fleet is so strong in ships and guns that if it engaged our fleet and was properly fought, it might be a very serious thing for us to have to fight a fleet of equal strength on the following day. But the question is: Would it be properly fought? Would the conscript German navy get as much out of their ships and guns as they ought? They have not ventured on any engagement, either with the English fleet or the much weaker Russian fleet, and their single ships have given our single ships a very wide berth, and where they have had the misfortune to meet them, have run away. Any German cruiser which wishes to bear out the "assumption-of-risk" theory has only to wait for an English cruiser, and she can have her "duel à l'outrance," and there is not an officer in the German navy who does not know this, and probably not a ship in the German navy which does not carry orders never to engage an English ship of anything like equal strength, for all the "assumption-of-risk" theory so magnanimously printed here. The German seamen may be "eager to win for the fleet such glory that it can be favorably contrasted with the deeds of the old and new armies," but their admirals and captains have never sought an action in the whole existence of the German navy, and the German fleet has not ventured into the North Sea since the beginning of the war.[1]

Contrary to general expectation, the German fleet has taken the offensive, and the first loss of the war is on the English side and in English waters, the English cruiser *Amphion* running on to German mines in the mouth of the Thames.

The idea of glory held by the writers of this book may be as distant from ours as their idea of taking the offensive. Our idea of taking the offensive is to come out and look for some one to fight—not to strew mines in the open sea, more dangerous to innocent vessels employed in commerce or fishing than to men-of-war, which keep a look-out. This we put on a par with poisoning wells. Three of our smaller cruisers have, it is true, been blown up by these mines, but the men who laid them are not naval warriors but dastards of exactly the same class as the man who threw the land-bomb which killed the Archduke Francis Ferdinand.[2]

Neither do we consider it taking the offensive for a battle cruiser like the " Goeben " to bom-

---

[1] Except the *Königsberg*, 3350 tons, which, receiving information from a spy that the *Pegasus*, 2135 tons, with guns of inferior range, was lying at anchor, steam-down, cleaning her boilers out and otherwise repairing, came in and put her out of action from a safe distance.

[2] As this goes to press there is news of a really brilliant dash by German submarines which resulted in the torpedoing of three armored cruisers.

bard towns on the Algerian coast as defenceless as Brighton and Margate.

In the Baltic and the Mediterranean also German ships have taken the offensive against the enemies' coast, as is shown by the bombardment by the Germans of the war harbor of Libau and of fortified landing-places on the Algerian coast.

When the "Goeben" and the "Breslau" heard that England had declared war, they ceased to confide in the "risk idea," and steamed east as hard as they could, presumably to make the Adriatic. They did not take advantage of the glorious opportunity of risk and serving their country presented by the fact that a French army was being transported from Algeria to France. When Nelson was chasing the transports which carried Napoleon's army and the fleet which convoyed them, he told off four ships to engage the entire French fleet until the others had sunk the transports. The "Goeben" and the "Breslau," if they had been animated by such a spirit, might have destroyed thousands of soldiers as well as inflicted great damage on the English men-of-war which guarded the crossing, before they were sunk, and they would have set the German navy the example of "confiding in the risk idea" which it seems to need so badly. But they took advantage of the English men-of-war being busy and fled. Headed off the Adriatic by small English ships—the boastful Austrian navy declined to come out and help them—they ran into Messina. Italian neutrality was strict, and in twenty-four hours they came out again, after leaving their wills and their valuables with their consul. They came out with their bands playing, talking about death and glory, and the world, which did not know how little they meant, was thrilled with admiration. But the British fleet was not there: was it still convoying the French army across the Mediterranean? there was only the little "Gloucester," about a match for the "Breslau" (in armament, two six-inch and ten four-inch guns, in speed twenty-six knots). Though the "Goeben" carried ten eleven-inch guns and was two knots faster, they did not turn and rend her, but fled before her to Constantinople. She hung on right up to the Dardanelles, chasing and shelling them—they passed in, and after holding up enemies' merchant ships in neutral waters, were saved by being sold to Turkey, crews and all.

And this veracious book was published after the inglorious exit of the "Goeben."

Thus the fleet, confiding in the "risk" idea now proved to be true, and in its earnest and courageous spirit, may look forward with confidence to coming events.

But will not civilians have to hunger and thirst in these days? That is an earnest question. The answer is, No. Even in Berlin, city of millions, the milk supply did not fail for a day. Infants will not have to bear the privations of war. All provisions are to be had at reasonable prices. Empire, municipalities, and merchants are working successfully together to ensure that there shall be a sufficient food supply at not too great a cost. Not only is our great army mobilized, but the whole folk is mobilized, and the distribution of labor, the food question, and the care of the sick and wounded are all being provided for. The whole German folk has become a gigantic war camp. All are mobilized to protect Kaiser, Folk, and Fatherland, as the closing report of the Reichstag puts it. And all Germany pays the tribute of a salute to the chiefs of the army and navy, who work with deeds, not words.

If this is true of Berlin, Berlin is more fortunate than Hamburg.

From the "Pall Mall Gazette," 14th September, 1914:

" Rome, Monday.

"Terrible stories are published here of the dearth of food in Germany, which is rapidly assuming a position of the extremest gravity.

"To all intents and purposes famine prevails in Hamburg, and a gentleman who was recently in that city, and who is now in Rome, asserts that the situation there is merely an example of the conditions prevailing all over Germany.

"He says that the immense storehouses in Hamburg, in which vast quantities of food had accumulated, have been taken over by the General Staff, and their contents have been sent to the front to be distributed among the troops.

"Traffic in Hamburg has ceased, and all factories closed. There are 1500 ships lying idle in the harbor, and the crews are suffering from hunger. Prices have risen to such an extent that even in the middle of August eggs cost ten marks a dozen.

"Fresh meat was unprocurable, all the cattle having been requisitioned. There was a very small quantity of milk and butter, but it had all been reserved for the hospitals. There was neither milk nor prepared food for babies, and long, sad processions of mothers could be seen outside the Town Hall imploring the City Fathers for assistance."—*Reuter*.

Possibly in Berlin there is someone of influence, such as the Empress, not deaf to the voice of humanity—the cry of the coming race from its cradle.

FOREWORD TO CHAPTER V

LLOYD GEORGE ON THE GERMAN EMPEROR IN HIS GREAT
SPEECH AT THE QUEEN'S HALL.

"Have you read the Kaiser's speeches? If you have not a copy,
I advise you to buy it; they will soon be out of print—and you
won't have any more of the same sort again. (Laughter and
cheers.) They are full of the clatter and bluster of German
militarists—the mailed fist, the shining armor. Poor old mailed
fist—its knuckles are getting a little bruised. Poor shining armor—the shine is being knocked out of it. (Laughter.) But
there is the same swagger and boastfulness running through the
whole of the speeches. You saw that remarkable speech which
appeared in the *British Weekly* this week. It is a very remarkable
product, as an illustration of the spirit we have got to fight. It
is his speech to his soldiers on the way to the front.

> Remember that the German people are the chosen of God.
> On me, on me as German Emperor, the Spirit of God has
> descended. I am His weapon, His sword, and His Vice-
> gerent. Woe to the disobedient. Death to cowards and
> unbelievers.

There has been nothing like it since the days of Mahomet.
Lunacy—(laughter)—is always distressing, but sometimes it is
dangerous, and when you get it manifested in the head of the
State and it has become the policy of a great empire it is about
time it should be ruthlessly put away. (Cheers.) I do not
believe he meant all these speeches, it was simply the martial
straddle which he had acquired. But there were men around him
who meant every word of it. This was their religion:—Treaties:
they tangle the feet of Germany in her advance; cut them with
the sword. Little nations: they hinder the advance of Germany;
trample them in the mire under the German heel. The Russian
Slav; he challenges the supremacy of Germany in Europe; hurl

88

your legions at him and massacre him. Britain: she is a constant menace to the predominancy of Germany in the world; wrest the trident out of her hand.

"More than that, the new philosophy of Germany is to destroy Christianity—sickly sentimentalism about sacrifice for others, poor pap for German mouths. We will have the new diet, we will force it on the world. It will be made in Germany—(laughter)—a diet of blood and iron. What remains? Treaties have gone; the honor of nations gone; liberty gone. What is left? Germany—Germany is left—*Deutschland über Alles*. That is all that is left. That is what we are fighting, that claim to predominancy of a civilization, a material one, a hard one, a civilization which, if once it rules and sways the world, liberty goes, democracy vanishes, and unless Britain comes to the rescue with her sons, it will be a dark day for humanity. (Loud cheers.)

"We are not fighting the German people. The German people are just as much under the heel of this Prussian military caste, and more so, thank God, than any other nation in Europe. It will be a day of rejoicing for the German peasant and artisan and trader when the military caste is broken. (Cheers.) You know his pretensions. He gives himself the airs of a demigod walking the pavement—civilians and their wives swept into the gutter; they have no right to stand in the way of the great Prussian Junker. Men, women, nations—they have all got to go. He thinks all he has got to say is, "We are in a hurry." (Laughter.) That is the answer he gave to Belgium. "Rapidity of action is Germany's greatest asset," which means, "I am in a hurry. Clear out of my way." You know the type of motorist, the terror of the roads, with a 60-h.p. car. He thinks the roads are made for him, and anybody who impedes the action of his car by a single mile is knocked down. The Prussian Junker is the road-hog of Europe. (Loud cheers.) Small nationalities in his way hurled to the roadside, bleeding and broken; women and children crushed under the wheels of his cruel car; Britain ordered out of his road. All I can say is this. If the old British spirit is alive in British hearts that bully will be torn from his seat. (Prolonged cheers.) Were he to win it would be the greatest catastrophe that befell democracy since the days of the Holy Alliance and its ascendancy."

CHAPTER V

ARMY AND NAVY

THE GERMAN ARMY AND NAVY ON THE WATCH—
FOUR MILLION GERMAN MEN IN THE FIELD—
THOUSANDS OF VOLUNTEERS JOIN THE COLORS
TO FIGHT FOR GERMANY'S EXISTENCE, AMONG
THEM THE FLOWER OF HER SCIENTIFIC AND
ARTISTIC LIFE.

THERE can be no greater contrast than that
between the United States and Germany in
one of the most important questions of existence
with which a state is confronted. In its whole
history the United States has never had a foreign,
a hostile force of invaders upon its territory;
foreign armies have never laid waste its fields.

> This is a tactful way of insinuating to the United
> States that they do not know what War means.
> But their great Civil War, which lasted over the
> first half of the sixties, gave them as searching a
> test as any war of modern times.

Until late in the last century, however, Germany
was the battlefield for the then most powerful

nations of Europe. The numerous German states and provinces, too, fought among themselves, often on behalf of foreign powers. The European great powers of that day were able, unhindered and unpunished, to take for themselves piece after piece of German territory. In the United States, on the other hand, it was years before the steadily increasing population attained to the boundaries set for it by nature.

Our Bismarck was finally able, in the years from 1864 to 1871, to create a great empire from the many small German states. As he himself often remarked, however, this was only possible because his policies and diplomacy rested upon and were supported by a well-trained and powerful army.

It is well that Germany confesses that Bismarck's policies and diplomacy rested on a large and well-trained army. The army wags Prussia, and Prussia wags Germany. If it had not been under the heel of the army would Bavaria have consented to the present war? Would Hamburg have voted for it?—Hamburg, which has fifteen hundred ships lying idle in its docks, and less seaborne trade than many an African village! The Prussian Prætorians, headed unfortunately by their Emperor, have drenched Europe with blood to extend the area of their tyrannies.

Nothing but the army is left of the Bismarckian policy. Would Bismarck have kept Alsace and Lorraine loyal to France by senseless persecutions? Would Bismarck have allowed Germany to go into the war with the whole civilized world

except Austria ready to league against her?
Would Bismarck have so gone to war that Italy
could within the terms of the Triple Alliance re-
fuse to join in on Germany's side? Would
Bismarck have consented to a plan of campaign
which was bound to make the unwilling English
Radicals declare war on Germany with the ardor
of jingoes? Would Bismarck have forgotten to
ascertain whether Japan would display an attitude
which would liberate large Russian armies from
Asia?—Japan, which since she came into the war
has sold to Russia her formidable siege-guns!

How the German Empire came into being at
that time is well known. A war was necessary
because the then so powerful France did not desire
that North and South Germany should unite.
She was not able to prevent this union, was defeated, and had to give back to us two old German
provinces which she had stolen from the Germans.
The old Field-Marshal von Moltke said not long
after the War of 1870–71, that the Germans would
still have to defend Alsace-Lorraine for fifty years
more. Perhaps he little realized how prophetic
his words were; but he and those who followed him,
the German emperors and the German war ministers, prepared themselves for this coming defensive struggle, and unremittingly devoted their
attention to the German army.

Moltke was born a Dane, and therefore in a
position to judge how strong were the feelings of

provinces made captive by Germany. He also knew the Prussian officer, and how impossible his brutalities would make the conciliation of any captive province. He foresaw Zabern and might have prophesied Louvain.

The principal preparation made by Germany for the present "defensive" struggle has lain, as one of our Under-Secretaries of State has well pointed out, in the preparation of siege-trains with gigantic guns for the invasion of France and Belgium.

From 1887 on there had been no doubt that in the event of war with France we should have to reckon also with Russia. This meant that the army must be strong enough to be equal to the coming fight on two borders—a tremendous demand upon the resources of a land when one considers that a peaceful folk, devoted to agriculture, industry, and trade, must live for decades in the constant expectation of being obliged, be it to-morrow, be it in ten years, to fight for its life against its two great military neighbors simultaneously. There are, moreover, the great money expenditures, and also the burden of universal military service, which, as is well known, requires every able-bodied male German to serve a number of years with the colors, and later to hold himself ready, first as a reservist, then as member of the Landwehr, and finally as member of the Landsturm, to spring to arms at the call of his supreme war lord, the German Emperor.

The men who in 1875 planned the war of extirpation against France when she began to recover from the War of 1870 were responsible for the Franco-Russian Alliance. It showed Prince Gortchakoff and the Czar Alexander what the invasion of Belgium has shown in the present war —that the policy of Germany is expressed by the naked cynicism of von Bernhardi's " Conditions may arise which are more powerful than the most honorable intentions." The same sentiment has been defined with yet more naked shamelessness by the German Chancellor, von Bethmann-Hollweg,—in his dictum that " a treaty is only a scrap of paper."

Germany's insecurity in living between two powerful and hostile neighbors was nothing in the opinion of Russia to the insecurity of living next door to a country with the politics of a brigand. As the brigand preys upon unsuspecting travelers, Germany was looking out for the opportunity to prey on unsuspecting neighbors. Hence the Franco-Russian Alliance, but for which Germany might have fallen on Russia's rear while she was fighting Japan.

As for the financial burden, by abandoning her designs against England, Germany could have done without an important navy. Until the Kaiser's telegram to Kruger England's navy was on the side of Germany. Germany's navy is part of her equipment as a brigand.

A warlike, militant nation would not long have endured such conditions, but would have compelled a war and carried it through swiftly. As

Bismarck said, however, the German army, since it is an army of the folk itself, is not a weapon for frivolous aggression. Since the German army, when it is summoned to war, represents the whole German people, and since the whole German people is peaceably disposed, it follows that the army can only be a defensive organization.

The book suggests that if Germany had not been a peaceful nation, she would have gone to war long ago to disarm other nations, after which she might have disarmed herself, unless she preferred to remain armed, forcing the unarmed rest of Europe to pay for her armaments. But it is not good policy for the most peaceful nation to declare wars for the conquest of her neighbors until opportunities make her success a certainty. Besides, if the German army were a purely defensive organization which would only be used to repel foreign aggression (and it must be remembered that the third member of the Triple Alliance refused to fight on the ground that this is purely a war of aggression), how could it have made such a war?

The fact is, that this peaceful nation, with an army purely for defensive purposes, has several times thrown down the glove, and reaped substantial advantages by the challenged nation not daring to pick it up. It must have been absolutely staggered when Great Britain, whom for once she was courting instead of challenging, instantly accepted war rather than betray her honor.

If war comes, millions of Germans must go to the front, must leave their parents, their families, their children. They *must*. And this "must" means not only the command of their Emperor, but also the necessity to defend their own land. Did not this necessity exist, these sons, husbands, and fathers would assuredly not go gladly to the battlefield, and it is likewise certain that those who stayed at home would not rejoice so enthusiastically to see them go as we Germans have seen them rejoicing in these days. Again, then, let us repeat that the German army is a weapon which can be and is used only for defense against foreign aggressions. When the aggressions come, the whole German folk stands with its army, as it does now.

But aggressions come when the Kaiser orders them. He has only to give the word to Austria as he gives the word to Hammann for a campaign of lies against England in the Press and the " amour propre " of the nation insulted by Austria may be trusted to do the rest. The German people does not appear to be able to distinguish between manufactured and spontaneous aggressions. Or perhaps it does and is only grinning like a plucky boy who is going to be caned, when writers like the author of this book are explaining to the mocking American that this is a purely democratic and defensive war. It seems a pity not to add that it has the approval of the Salvation Army.

The German army is divided into twenty-five corps in times of peace. In war-times reservists, members of the Landwehr, and occasionally also of the Landsturm are called to the colors. The result is that the German army on a war footing is a tremendously powerful organ.

Quite an important addition to its numbers can be made by calling in the German spies who are stationed in other countries.

Our opponents in foreign countries have for years consistently endeavored to awaken the belief that the German soldier does his obligatory service very unwillingly, that he does not get enough to eat and is badly treated. These assertions are false, and anybody who has seen in these weeks of mobilization how our soldiers, reservists and Landwehr men, departed for the field or reported at the garrisons, anybody who has seen their happy, enthusiastic, and fresh faces, knows that mishandled men, men who have been drilled as machines, cannot present such an appearance.

If the German soldier is not badly treated by his officers, he is a sad liar. For the books which deal with such subjects, in Germany as elsewhere, are full of his woes. In the present war great numbers of German prisoners have wounds at the backs of their legs and feet which they allege that they have received from the swords and revolvers of their officers, who march behind

7

them and drive them into action in solid masses,
which carried them to the gates of Paris, though
by the hundred thousand men are said to have
fallen by the way. Presuming that they are very
well fed under ordinary circumstances, one may
note that from the time that they crossed the
Belgian frontier the German commissariat arrangements for food have broken down.

On the day the German mobilization was
ordered we travelled with some Americans from
the western border to Berlin. These Americans
said: "We do not know much about your army,
but judging by what we have seen in these days,
there prevails in it and all its arrangements such
system that it must win. System must win every
time." In this saying there is, indeed, much of
truth—order and system are the basis upon which
the mighty organization of our army is built.

The enormous masses of men which Germany
was able to throw upon Belgium within a few
days of the beginning of the war show, even if
some secret system of mobilization had been in
operation, the wonderful organization of the
German army. They were able to send out two
million or more men, wonderfully complete in
armament and transport, even if they left the
provisioning, or some of it, to the chances of what
they could requisition in the occupied countries.
But the American who said that " system must
win every time " was ignorant of a truth still more
axiomatic in war—that where both sides are well

organized, generalship and personal ascendancy are prime factors, and that where the generalship is pretty equal and the numbers are pretty equal, one nation may completely dominate another in battle. Apparently, though the officers are a military people, the men of the German army are not. The enormous heroism they have shown, the enormous military feats which they have accomplished in marching to the gates of Paris are due to discipline and training, and above all to their exalted love of the Fatherland, which enables them to face terrible and hellish situations to which they have no berserking spirit to impel them. The individual German " Tommy " does not want to " go for " the individual English " Tommy " as the individual English " Tommy " wants to go for him.

Now a word concerning the German officer. He, too, has been much maligned; he is often misunderstood by foreigners, and yet we believe that the people of the United States in particular must be able to understand the German officer. One of the greatest sons of free America, George Washington, gave his countrymen the advice to select only gentlemen as officers, and it is according to this principle that the officers of the German army and navy are chosen. Their selection is made, moreover, upon a democratic basis, in that the officers' corps of the various regiments decide for themselves whether they will or will not accept as a comrade the person whose name is proposed to them.

The people in the United States have been very explicit about the German officer. We English trust that German officers as a class have been maligned. We are unwilling to believe that the estimate can be true of them generally; we are unwilling to believe that the picture drawn of them in " Life in a Garrison Town " is typical, true as it may be of the particular regiment in which the author was a lieutenant. There German officers are made out to be drunken, bestial, caddish, dishonest, not even particularly brave, and, of course, abominably arrogant. We know, in spite of what Lieutenant Bilse has written, that the German army must be full of officers who are brave gentlemen as well as born aristocrats. We have heard innumerable instances of the noble manners of the best of them in their intercourse with foreigners. If they are arrogant to their men it is because it is the tradition of their service. If they drink heavily, it is because popular opinion does not condemn it, and it must be remembered that they rarely drink spirits, except in the form of " petits verres." " A drink " in Germany does not mean a whiskey-and-soda. The openness of their " amours " would in England be a public scandal, and in America would lead to wholesale murder. In connection with it, credit must be given to the German authorities for the measures taken to stamp out a disease which is infinitely more dangerous to the community than hydrophobia.

The other side of the shield is a bright one. The German officer is devoted to the study of his profession, and has carried military science to a higher degree than had ever been known before.

The rest of the paragraph will seem to Americans almost comical. George Washington would be hooted all over America if he advised the American of to-day to " select only gentlemen as officers." West Point is absolutely democratic as to the candidates who may submit themselves for the army entrance examination, though it turns out such a splendid article. To allow the officers of a regiment to blackball a man who has been appointed to their regiment would not strike an Englishman or an American as democratic, but as rank snobbery.

One sees that the German army is not, as many say, a tremendous machine, but rather a great, living organism, which draws its strength and life-blood from all classes of the whole German folk. The German army can develop its entire strength only in a war which the folk approve, that is, when a defensive war has been forced upon them. That this is true, will have been realized by our friends in the United States before this comes into their hands.

The description " a great living organism, which draws its strength and life-blood from all classes of the whole German folk " is, from the literary point of view, unfortunate. It is too like the definition of a vampire, which is the American view of the German army, as well as our own. The statement that " the German army can develop its entire strength only in a war which the folk approve " will strike the rest of the world as a gloomy prognostication of defeat. One asks aghast: Did the German people, which had built up in forty years a manufacturing interest, an overseas commerce, a mercantile fleet rivaling those of England and the United States, really wish to start a war, in which all these, and even the German Empire itself, might be lost, just to enable Austria to punish Servia for a murder with which Servia may have had nothing to do, or to crush and rob Servia because she feared her?— Did the German people really, if all this talk of avenging the Archduke's murder and freeing Austria from the Servian menace was fudge, really wish to imperil everything dear to it in life, and a million German lives, just to humiliate Russia, and make the small nations regard her as a broken reed? If they did, history will record it as the most notorious instance of midsummer madness affecting a whole people. To use a homely business phrase, " It really was not good enough." But then, we have only the word of the egregious writer of this book's word for it, and we prefer to trust the German people.

The German fleet is in like manner a weapon of defense. It was very small up to the end of the last century, but has since then been consistently built up according to the ground principles which Mr. Roosevelt has so often in his powerful manner laid down for the American fleet. The question has often been asked, what is there for the German fleet to defend, since the German coast-line is so short? The answer is that the strength of a fleet must not be made to depend upon the length of coast-lines, but upon how many ships and how much merchandise go out from and enter the harbors, how great overseas interests there are, how large the colonies are and how they are situated, and finally how strong the sea-powers are with which Germany may have to carry on a war and how they are situated. To meet all these requirements there is but one remedy, namely, either that our fleet shall be strong enough to prevent the strongest sea-power from conducting war against us, or that, if war does come, it shall be able so to battle against the mightiest opponent that the latter shall be seriously weakened.

The theory that the German fleet is a weapon of defense would be a very plausible one if the hireling German professor, who corresponds to Dr. Hammann in the newspaper world, had not been at such pains to brag about the rapidity with which it was going to overhaul the British navy, and what it was going to do to it when the overhauling was complete. Otherwise, it would have seemed only patriotic and natural that Germany should amass a respectable fleet to be able to dispute the Monroe Doctrine, if her vital interests were assailed while she was establishing a new Germany in the south of Brazil, or if she happened to be at war with Russia, and wished to

prevent the Baltic becoming a Russian lake. A fleet up to the standard of France or Russia or Italy might have been classed as a weapon of defense. A fleet to make her equal the sea-power of England, which only kept up a very small army as a weapon of defense, could not fairly be classed in this category. No one disputes Germany's right to have such a fleet if she could afford it, but the Ballin-Bülow committee stultifies itself by taking the responsibility of a book which advances such foolish pretensions.

The latter part of the paragraph lets the real cat out of the bag. The fleet has to be equal to strong sea-powers " with which Germany may have to carry on war, and has to be so strong that the mightiest sea-power cannot fight it without being seriously weakened." If that is so, why this puerile blarney about it being intended only for purposes of defense?

Germany, as especially the Americans know, has become a great merchant marine nation, whose colonies are flourishing. Furthermore, since the land's growing population has greatly increased its strength in the course of the last years, the mistrust and jealousy of Great Britain have in particular been directed against the development of our ocean commerce, and later of our navy. To the upbuilding of the German navy were ascribed all manner of plans—to attack Great Britain, to make war on Japan, etc. It was even declared by the English press that Germany intended to attack the United States as soon as its fleet was strong enough. To-day, when Great Britain has needlessly declared war upon us, the Americans will perhaps believe that our fleet was never planned or built for an attack on anyone. Germany desired simply to protect its coasts and its marine interests *in the same manner in which it protects its land boundaries.* It is realized in the United States as well as here that a fleet can be powerful only when it has a sufficient number of vessels of all classes, and when it is thoroughly and unremittingly schooled in times of peace. We have tried to attain this ideal in Germany, and it may be remarked that the training of the personnel requires greater efforts here, since the principle of universal service is also applied to the fleet, with a resulting short term of service, whereas all foreign fleets have a long term of enlistment.

That the German fleet was built for aggression against England or to frighten the United States from going to war against Germany for the enforcement of the Monroe Doctrine—that it was not built to protect its coasts and its marine interests, is amply shown by the fact that it has not been seen on the coast of the North Sea since the war began, and that it has not fought an action against a single British man-of-war (see page 82) to prevent German commerce being swept from the sea, though there are both English cruisers and German cruisers in the Atlantic and the Pacific. Under these circumstances, what on earth has it

to do with the idea of defense? Its sole aims are, if it gets the chance, to prey on British commerce or escort a German expedition to invade Great Britain. It must be admitted that it is a very scientifically designed navy, with excellent ships and guns, always kept on something like a war-footing. Its personnel is at present an unknown quantity.

The nominal strength of the German fleet is regulated by statute, as is also the term—twenty years—at the expiration of which old vessels must automatically be replaced by new ones. This fleet-strength is set at 41 line-of-battle ships, 20 armored cruisers, and 40 small cruisers, besides 144 torpedo-boats and 72 submarine vessels. These figures, however, have not been reached. To offset this fact, however, almost the whole German fleet has been kept together in home waters. Great Britain's fleet is much stronger than ours, but despite this, the German fleet faces its great opponent with coolness and assurance and with that courage and readiness to undertake great deeds that mark those who know that their land has been unjustifiably attacked.

I express no opinion as to how far the number of ships laid down in the schedule has been attained. That it has not been attained the Germans assure us in this book.

To say that the German fleet faces the British with "that courage and readiness to undertake great deeds that mark those who know that their

land has been unjustifiably attacked " does not
seem to English and Americans to have been
proved. The obvious fact is that the German
fleet has been ordered to keep out of harm's way,
bitterly, as one may imagine, to the disgust of the
bulk of the officers, "who work with deeds not
words."

It is utterly incorrect to say, as has been said,
that the German naval officers are filled with
hatred for other navies, especially for the British.
On the contrary, the relations between German
and English officers and men have always been
good, almost as good as those of the Germans with
the American officers. It is not personal hatred
that inspires our officers and men with the lust
for battle, but their indignation over the unpro-
voked attack and the realization that, if everyone
will do his best for the Fatherland in this great
hour, it will not be in vain even against the greatest
naval power. We, too, are confident of this, for
strenuous and faithful effort always has its reward,
and this is especially true of our fleet organization.

German naval officers are respected and popular with the officers of our own and other fleets.
But one could wish that the German Admiralty's
idea of " doing its best for the Fatherland in this
great hour " was not laying mines in open commercial waters, and skulking in forgotten harbors of South America and Africa until there is a
chance of falling on an unsuspecting merchant-
man. The "Dresden" and the "Karlsruhe"

and the " Leipzig " can have a light-weight boxing match with an English cruiser of the same size at sight.

The United States realizes this as well as we, for it, too, has built up a strong and admirably-trained fleet by prodigious labor. As is the case with the German fleet, the American navy is also not built for aggression, but for defense.

When the German fleet meets the American over a question involved by the Monroe Doctrine it will be amusing to hear what Americans have to say upon this point of aggression or defense.

FOREWORD TO CHAPTER VI

The Times, August 11th, 1914:

"As I find that the Chancellor's Reichstag speech of August 4th has not been published in England, I will give here the vital passage. After dealing with the diplomatic and military issues, the Imperial Chancellor said:

" 'Gentlemen, we are now in a state of necessity, and necessity knows no law! Our troops have occupied Luxemburg, and perhaps (as a matter of fact, the speaker knew that Belgium had been invaded that morning) are already on Belgian soil. Gentlemen, that is contrary to the dictates of international law. It is true that the French Government have declared at Brussels that France is willing to respect the neutrality of Belgium as long as her opponent respects it. We knew, however, that France stood ready for the invasion. France could wait, but we could not wait. A French movement upon our flank upon the Lower Rhine might have been disastrous. So we were compelled to override the just protest of the Luxemburg and Belgian Governments. The wrong—I speak openly—that we are committing we will endeavor to make good as soon as our military goal has been reached. Anybody who is threatened, as we are threatened, and is fighting for his highest possessions, can have only one thought—how he is to hack his way through (*wie er sich durchhaut*).' "

Lloyd George in his Queen's Hall speech on English, French, and German neutrality:

"There is no man in this room who has always regarded the prospects of engaging in a great war with greater reluctance, with greater repugnance, than I have done throughout the whole of my political life. There is no man either inside or outside of this room more convinced that we could not have avoided it without national dishonor. (Cheers.) I am fully alive to the fact that whenever a nation has engaged in any war she has always invoked the sacred name of honor. Many a crime has been committed in its name; there are some crimes being committed now. But all the same, *national honor is a reality, and any nation that disregards it is doomed.* Why is our honor as a country involved in this war? Because in the first place we are bound in an honorable obligation to defend the independence, the liberty, the integrity of a small neighbor that has lived peaceably, but she could not have compelled us because she was weak. (Cries of 'Quite right!') *The man who declines to discharge his debt because his creditor is too poor to enforce it is a blackguard.* (Cheers.)

"We entered into this treaty, a solemn treaty, a full treaty, to defend Belgium and her integrity. Our signatures are attached to the document. Our signatures do not stand alone. This was not the only country to defend the integrity of Belgium. Russia, France, Austria, and Prussia—(hisses)—they are all there. Why did they not perform the obligation? It is suggested that this treaty is purely an excuse on our part. It is our low craft and cunning, just to cloak our jealousy of a superior civilization which we are attempting to destroy. Our answer is the action we took in 1870. Mr. Gladstone was then Prime Minister. Lord Granville, I think, was Foreign Secretary. I have never heard it alleged to their charge that they were ever jingoes. That treaty bond was this: we called upon the belligerent Powers to respect that treaty. We called upon France, we called upon Germany. At that time, bear in mind, the greatest danger to Belgium came from France and not from Germany. We intervened to protect Belgium against France exactly as we are doing now to protect her against Germany. We are proceeding exactly in the same way. We invited both the belligerent Powers to state that they had no intention of violating Belgian territory. *What was the answer given by Bismarck? He said it was superfluous to ask Prussia such a question in view of the treaties in force. France gave a similar answer.*

CHAPTER VI

NEUTRALITY BY THE GRACE OF ENGLAND

JANUS, a mighty god of the ancient Romans, was represented as having two faces. He could smile and frown simultaneously.

This god Janus is the personification of Neutrality according to English ideas. Neutrality smiles when violated by England and frowns when violated by other Powers.

> This epigram on England and neutrality is the one real achievement of this remarkable book. It is a bright, pithy saying which will please all the enemies of England. But considering the pains taken by England to avoid the violation of neutrality, even in the case of a German ship carrying weapons to the Boers during their war with England, it is easy for Neutrality to be gracious when England does make a slip.

The United States got a taste of England's neutrality when, a century ago, the English impressed thousands of American sailors, taking them from American ships on the high seas, when they searched neutral ships and confiscated the enemy's property on board of them, until Congress in Washington voted for the declaration of war against England.

In the great Civil War, 1861 to 1864, England had counted on the victory of the Southern States; she recognized them as belligerents and supplied them with warships. This was not considered by England a breach of neutrality until the minister of the United States declared, on September 5th, 1863, that unless England desisted, war would result. England yielded.

> If the writer of this book had had any knowledge of history or notions of fairness, he would have perceived that England's yielding was the finest possible example of her fairness and neutrality. She could have fought against the Northerners side by side with the Southern States without the smallest ultimate risk to herself. Her fleet throwing men and supplies into the Southern ports and her money would have turned the scale without the shadow of a doubt. But she resisted the temptation as she resisted the temptation to send the Russian admiral's fleet to the bottom when he fired upon the Grimsby trawlers (see page 116). All thinking Americans acknowledge her justice and magnanimity just as freely as the English acknowledge that it has been for the good of the world that the North did win.

But, according to the old German proverb: "A cat cannot resist catching mice," she secretly permitted the fitting out of privateers (the *Ala-*

bama) for the Southern States and was finally forced to pay an indemnity of $15,000,000. England gained, however, more than she lost by this interpretation of neutrality, for by the aid of her privateers American maritime trade passed into English hands and was lost to the Americans.

> **There are violations and violations. All violations of neutrality are not of the same class as the German invasion of Belgium. And when a violation of neutrality has been urged against England, she has shown a more commendable readiness to submit the matter to arbitration than any other nation. Of all the great Powers, England has stood longest and most ardently for the principle of arbitration, instead of demanding redress by arms. She submitted the celebrated "Alabama" claim alluded to above to arbitration, and paid the three millions damages accorded against her without any ill-feeling.**

"May God's vengeance fall on Germany! She has violated Belgium's neutrality!" the English piously ejaculate. They call themselves God's chosen people, the instrument of Providence for the benefit of the whole universe. They look down upon all other peoples with open, or silent, contempt, and claim for themselves various prerogatives, in particular the supremacy of the sea, even in American waters—from Jamaica to Halifax.

England's policy has always been to take all,

8

to give back nothing, to constantly demand more, to begrudge others everything. Only where the New World is concerned has England, conscious of her weakness, become less grasping, since Benjamin Franklin "wrested the scepter from the Tyrants," since the small colonies that fought so valiantly for their liberty rose to form the greatest dominion of the white race.

When Germany violated Belgian neutrality, England did not appeal to heaven in the blasphemous and patronizing language of the Kaiser. But though she was ruled at the time by a Government which has always urged consideration for Germany, and though she was willing to make any other sacrifice except the national honor for the maintenance of peace, she declared war. The sarcastic reference to England's attempted claim of the supremacy of the sea comes ill in a book issued by a committee with the chairman of the Hamburg-American Steamship Company at its head, for it is so undeniable that there is hardly a German ship, Hamburg-American or otherwise, afloat on the whole sea, except a few small cruisers and their colliers playing hide-and-seek. Nor is it very becoming in Germany to say that England's policy has always been to take all and give back nothing, for she gave Germany Heligoland, and its Bight, in return for a little island off the east coast of Africa, and Germany would not have her New Guinea Colony (if, indeed, she still has it and did not lose it with the Bismarck Islands, when they were conquered by the Aus-

tralian expedition) if Great Britain had not
made Queensland give it up a short time before.

In the summer of 1911, during the Franco-
German-Morocco dispute, the English were determined to assist their old enemies the French
against Germany, and stationed 160,000 troops
along their coast, ready for embarkation. For
the French coast? No indeed! For transporta-
tion to Antwerp, where the English were to unite
with the French army and combine in the destruction of the German forces. But things did not
reach that stage. England was not ready. England and France were resolved not to respect the
neutrality of Belgium—that same England that
solemnly assures the world that she has never at
any time or place committed a breach of neutrality. England has observed neutrality only when
compatible with her own interests, which has not
often been the case. Her whole dissimulating
policy is much more questionable than our one
breach of neutrality, committed in self-defense
and accompanied by the most solemn promises
of indemnity and restitution.

**This is a deliberate mis-statement. Not a man
was moved. These troops could only have been
sent at the request of Belgium, and not at the
request of France. Belgium would have been
very glad to have them at the outbreak of the
present war, and it would have been a very good
thing from the Belgian point of view.
It is not true that England has observed neu-**

trality only when compatible with her own interests, or Germany would never have had the Kiel Canal. If England had consulted her own interests, she would obviously have prevented the dismemberment of Denmark. And when England did not sink the Russian fleet which had fired on the Grimsby trawlers as it was making its way to Japan, all the world wondered at our maintaining our neutrality, for Russia had been our persistent enemy in Asia and was actually at war with Japan, England's Ally, though we were not bound to support Japan with arms unless a second power attacked her. Such a phrase as "her whole dissimulating policy" is much more applicable to Germany than England. Germany was pretending to do her best to maintain peace when she had given directions to Austria to make war inevitable. England was honestly straining every nerve to have peace maintained, and all the chancelleries of Europe knew as well as they knew their A B C that if war happened, the British Government knew that it was its duty, and necessary to its self-preservation, to fight on the side of France, but that the majority of the party in power was against England's going to war if war could be honorably avoided. Germany was especially conscious of it, and traded on it.

Mr. Lloyd George, in his great Queen's Hall speech of September 19th, has told us in very plain English the true story of Germany's violation of Belgian neutrality:

Just look at the interview which took place between our Ambassador and great German officials. When their attention was called to this treaty to which they were parties they said: "We cannot help that." Rapidity of action was the great German asset. There is a greater asset for a nation than rapidity of action, and that is honest dealing. (Cheers.) What are her excuses? She says that Belgium was plotting against her; that Belgium was engaged in a great conspiracy with Britain and with France to attack her. Not merely is it not true, but Germany knows it is not true. What is her other excuse? France meant to invade Germany through Belgium. Absolutely untrue. France offered Belgium five Army Corps to defend her if she were attacked. Belgium said: "I don't require them, I have got the word of the Kaiser. *Shall Caesar send a lie?*"

England and France did not give up their plan of attacking Germany through Belgium, and by this means won the approval of the Muscovites. Three against one! It would have been a crime against the German people if the German General Staff had not anticipated this intention. The inalienable right of self-defense gives the individual, whose very existence is at stake, the moral liberty to resort to weapons which would be forbidden except in times of peril. As Belgium would, nevertheless, not acquiesce in a friendly neutrality which would permit the unobstructed passage of German troops through small portions of her territory, although her integrity was guaranteed, the German General Staff was obliged to force this passage in order to avoid the necessity of meeting the enemy on the most unfavorable ground.

This is one of the most disingenuous paragraphs in a book whose whole purpose is to

deceive. There was no question of England and France trying to win the approval of the Muscovites. Russia was the Power attacked, and Germany was attacking her. The whole conduct of the war shows that England and France could have had no idea of attacking Germany through Belgium because they were so unprepared for the contingency that, when they had Belgium on their side, and all her fortresses open to them, they had no plans ready to take their advantage, while the Germans had every yard of their march through Belgium planned out. To say that " the inalienable right of self-defense gives the individual whose every existence is at stake the moral liberty to resort to weapons which would be forbidden except in times of peril," applies to the man whose house is burgled, not to the burglar. Germany was unfortunately the burglar, who, if he carries a Browning pistol, as a rule does so without making any pious excuses.

The contention that Germany had a right to force the passage of Belgium because Belgium would not consent to her neutrality being violated is the most impudent piece of treaty-breaking since the world began. Von Bernhardi has not lived in vain.

The Germans have not forgotten the tone in which the French and Belgian press reported the frequent excursions of French Staff officers and Generals for the purpose of making an exhaustive study of the territory through which the armies are now moving, and who were received with open arms in Belgium and treated like brothers. Belgium has become the vassal of France.

This is merely the German way of stating that French officers were frequently present at Belgian maneuvers. So were German officers. General French had the same opportunities of an exhaustive study of German territory when he was present at the German maneuvers. It is throwing dust in people's eyes to talk of Belgium having become the vassal of France. Sir Edward Grey demanded from France a promise that she would respect the neutrality of Belgium as categorical as the promise he demanded from Germany. In essentials the dispatches were identical. France gave it; and that France meant what she said has never been disputed, and cannot be.

It was in this connection that Mr. Lloyd George made one of the finest points of his great Queen's Hall speech—that France could have avoided the surrender at Sedan by violating Belgian territory.

The French Army was wedged up against the Belgian frontier, every means of escape shut up by a ring of flame from Prussian cannon. There was one way of escape—by violating the neutrality of Belgium. The French on that occasion preferred ruin and humiliation to the breaking of their bond. The French Emperor, French marshals, 100,000 gallant Frenchmen in arms, preferrred to be carried captive to the strange land of their enemy rather than dishonor the name of their country. It was the last French Army defeat. Had they violated Belgian neutrality the whole history of that war would have been changed. And yet it was the interest of France to break the treaty. She did not do it. It is the interest of Prussia to break the treaty, and she has done it. ("Shame.") She avowed it with cynical contempt for every principle of justice. She says treaties only bind you when it is to your interest to keep them. What is a treaty? says the German Chancellor. "A scrap of paper." Have you any five-pound notes about you? I am not calling for them. (Laughter.) Have you any of those neat little Treasury one-pound notes? (Laughter.) If you have, burn them; they are only scraps of paper. (Cheers.) What are they made of? Rags. (Laughter.) What are they worth? The whole credit of the *British* Empire. (Cheers.)

In our place the Government of the United States would not have acted differently. "Inter arma silent leges" —in the midst of arms the laws are silent. Besides, England had interfered beforehand in Germany's plan of campaign by declaring that she would not tolerate an attack upon the northern coast of France.

To say that President Wilson, with his international jurist's mind, would have violated Belgian neutrality as Germany did, would be an insult to the United States if it were not so ludicrous, and only the country of von Bernhardi would have pleaded as an excuse for violating Belgium's neutrality that England had interfered beforehand in Germany's plan of campaign by declaring that she would not tolerate an attack upon the northern coast of France. What would President Wilson say to this? What on earth had it to do with Belgium ?

The German troops, with their iron discipline, will respect the personal property and liberty of the individual in Belgium, just as they did in France in 1870.

This passage is one of the outstanding features of Germany's appeal to posterity conveyed in the eighty-six pages of " Truth about Germany; Facts about the War."

The destruction of Louvain is an instance of this " iron discipline." The common soldiers are understood to have been appalled by it, but submitted to the orders of their general and their officers. It and the atrocities submitted by the Belgian Government to the President of the United States form the subject of an appendix at the end of this chapter.

Mr. Lloyd George in his Queen's Hall speech, said:

Belgium has been treated brutally—how brutally we shall not yet know. We know already too much. What had she done? Had she sent an ultimatum to Germany? Had she challenged Germany? Was she preparing to make war on Germany? Had she inflicted any wrong upon Germany which the Kaiser was bound to redress? She was one of the most unoffending little countries in Europe. There she was peaceable, industrious, thrifty, hardworking, giving offense to no one. Her cornfields have been trampled down. Her villages have been burned to the ground. Her art treasures have been destroyed. Her men have been slaughtered; yes, and her women and her children too. What had she done? Hundreds and thousands of her people, their neat, comfortable little homes burnt to the dust, wandering homeless in their own land. What was their crime? Their crime was that they trusted to the word of a Prussian King.

I am not depending on them (*i. e.*, the Belgians). It is enough for me to have the story which the Germans them-

selves avow, admit, defend, proclaim. The burning and
massacring, the shooting down of harmless people. Why?
Because, according to the Germans, they fired on German
soldiers. What business had German soldiers there at all?
(Cheers.) Belgium was acting in pursuance of a most sacred
right, the right to defend your own home. But they were
not in uniform when they shot. If a burglar broke into the
Kaiser's palace at Potsdam, destroyed his furniture, shot
down his servants, ruined his art treasures, especially those
he made himself—(laughter and cheers)—burned his precious
manuscripts, do you think he would wait until he got into
uniform before he shot him down? (Laughter.) They were
dealing with those who had broken into their households.

Rheims Cathedral was one of the most precious heritages
of all mankind, as it did not belong to any individual; the
German troops, with their iron discipline, probably saw no
reason why they should respect it.

The Belgians would have been wise if they had
permitted the passage of the German troops.
They would have preserved their integrity, and
besides that, would have fared well from the
business point of view, for the army would have
proved a good customer and paid cash.

**The idea that the Belgians should put their
neutrality up to auction is in von Bernhardi's
best manner. He might have illustrated it with a
cartoon of Germany as the wolf making the suggestion to Belgium as Little Red Riding-Hood.**

**The suggestion here, " it may be dishonorable
but it will pay," is thoroughly German. Throughout there is no reference to the fact that by treaty
Belgium was bound to preserve her neutrality.**

Germany has always been a good and just
neighbor, to Belgium as well as to the other small

Powers such as Holland, Denmark, and Switzerland, which England in her place would have swallowed up one and all long ago.

It is difficult to understand why Belgium, Holland, and Denmark should have been less afraid of " their good and just neighbor," Germany, whose access to the sea they barred, than of England, who, had she possessed them, would have needed an army of four millions to defend her frontiers from " the good and just neighbor " in return for getting ports not so good as her own on the sea which she already dominates! It is inconceivable that England, if she had been in Germany's position, would have been such a fool as to knock her head against the stone wall of Switzerland. The idea of Germany being a good and just neighbor to Denmark, whom she robbed of Schleswig-Holstein and the site of the Kiel Canal, will strike the Americans, for whom the book was written, as very humorous. They will suspect " Count John Bernstorff " of having inspired this passage.

It does not appear that Holland's view of the good and just neighbor differs from that of Belgium and Denmark.

The development of industry on the lower Rhine has added to the prosperity of Belgium and has made Antwerp one of the first ports on the Continent, as well as one of the most important centers of exchange for German-American trade.

It may be admitted that German commerce has added greatly to the prosperity of Antwerp. Ant-

werp liked German commerce, but she liked
Germany so little that she made the fortifications
of Antwerp on the land side the most powerful in
Europe.

Without Germany Belgium could never have
acquired the Congo.

When England meditated taking possession of
the Congo, claiming that great rivers are nothing
but arms of the sea, and consequently belong to
the supreme maritime power, King Leopold turned
to Germany for protection and received it from
Bismarck, who called the Congo Conference of
1884–5 and obtained the recognition by the Powers
of the independence of the Congo State.

England certainly never made any such pre-
posterous claim.

If Germany did assist, not Belgium, but the
late King of the Belgians, to acquire the Congo
State, it was only because Belgium was a small
Power from whom, in the fullness of time, she
would be able to steal the Congo, even if she did
not steal Belgium with it. England was a great
Power, with such a gigantic fleet that there was
no chance of stealing any colonies from her until
she was herself conquered.

The struggle of the German States in Europe
has some points in common with the struggle of
the Independent States of North America (from
1778 to 1783), for it is directed chiefly against

England's scheming guardianship, and her practice of weakening the Continental Powers by sowing or fostering dissension among them.

It is one of the prize lies in the collection to say that the Austro-German Alliance is " directed chiefly against England's scheming guardianship and her practice of weakening the Continental Powers by sowing or fostering dissension among them." It is universally recognized that no one has worked harder for a concert of Europe than Sir Edward Grey, and all through the Balkan crisis he worked successfully, though under great difficulties. The Triple Alliance of Germany, Austria, and Italy was formed because Germany was afraid of Russia, which she perceived would become too powerful if allied to a strong France. The sympathies of England were at the time with Germany, and were wantonly alienated by the present Kaiser. Until 1911, when Mr. Lloyd George uttered his warning over the second Morocco incident, any German military politician would have screamed with contemptuous laughter at the idea of England having the pluck to fight about anything, or the sense to stand by her friends. Until last month Germany regarded the possibility of England's interference as negligible.

There is only one resemblance between the present war and the American War of Independence, and that is that England lost then because most of the rest of the world was leagued against her power over the sea, as most of the rest of the world is now leagued against Germany's hegemony.

While continually protesting her love of peace, England has carried on no fewer than forty wars during the latter half of the nineteenth century, including the great Boer War. She has long imperilled, and in the end has succeeded in disturbing, the peace of Europe by her invidious policy of isolating Germany. Germany, on the other hand, has proved herself since 1871 to be the strongest and most reliable security for the peace of Europe.

> It is true that England had many wars in the last half of the nineteenth century, but none of them, except the Crimean War, were of her own seeking, and of the others only the South African and Indian Mutinies were of any great importance.
>
> To say that she has long imperilled the peace of Europe by her policy of isolating Germany, since Germany's attempt to make a coalition with Russia and France against her, is to turn the truth inside out. Nothing but the knowledge that King Edward VII. had arranged an entente of nearly all non-Teutonic Europe (including Italy, which was nominally the ally of the Teutonic Powers) kept Germany from going to war with first this State and then the other to rob them of provinces as she had robbed France and Denmark. When German military brigandage has once been extinguished, there will be peace in Europe for fifty years.

The policy of sowing dissension, practised by England more industriously than ever in recent years, cannot possibly meet with the approval of the peace-loving citizens of the United States, and should be condemned on merely humanitarian as well as commercial grounds.

> "The peace-loving citizens of the United States" know better than anyone else how anxious Great Britain has been to refer every international trouble to arbitration. They know that Sir Edward Gr:y went so far as to offer to make a General Peace Treaty with the U. S. A. They know that Germany, if she were powerful enough to bully the United States and at the same time keep her powder dry for Europe, would upset the Monroe Doctrine to-morrow to establish German colonies in South America, and they will see no humanitarian reasons for being suspicious of England, who is watching the brigand in Europe.

England aims at being mistress of the Old World in order to occupy either an equal, or a menacing, position towards the New World, as circumstances may dictate. For this purpose she has encouraged this war. The German Federated States of Europe are defending themselves with might and main, and are counting in this struggle for existence on the goodwill of the United States of America, for whose citizens they cherish the friendliest feelings, as they have proved at all times. All Americans who have visited Germany will surely bear witness to that effect.

> Nothing is further from England than aiming at a hegemony of the continent of Europe. When

she owned half France as well as the British
Islands from the twelfth to the fifteenth century,
she never once invaded what is now Germany.
And her historians are unanimous in the contention that losing her possessions in France gave
England her position in the world. She has not
the slightest wish to be the mistress of the Old
World, except as regards the southern peninsula
of Asia, known generally as India. She desires
absolute peace in Europe, absolute detachment
from Europe in all matters except commerce, in
order to be the center of a great Imperial Federa-
tion of Colonies.

Germany is as aware of this as America is, and
she knows that a man has to be as mad as the
drowned King of Bavaria to imagine that England
has the smallest design at the expense of the
United States. Americans will hardly believe
their senses when they read that a representative
committee of Germans like Prince Bülow, Field-
Marshal von der Goltz, Count Reventlow, and the
heads of the Hamburg-American and the North
German Lloyd Steamship Companies and the
Deutsche Bank, have seriously allowed a book to
go forth under their names, which suggests that
England has got up this war in Europe with a view
to attacking the United States afterwards. The
poor attacked Germany and Austria, who really
precipitated this war so deliberately, advance this
tomfoolery as a reason why the United States
should extend them their active sympathy in the
struggle. The American will enjoy his character
for simplicity.

APPENDIX—ON THE GERMAN ATROCITIES AT LOUVAIN, DINANT, AERSCHOT, AND TERMONDE

THE Press Bureau issued this translation of the second report of the Belgian Commission of Inquiry on the violation of the Rights of Nations and of the Laws and Customs of War :

To MONS. CARTON DE WIART, MINISTER OF JUSTICE.

Antwerp, August 31st, 1914.

SIR,—The Commission of Inquiry have the honor to make the following report on acts of which the town of Louvain, the neighborhood and district of Malines have been the scene:

The German army entered Louvain on Wednesday, August 19th, after having burnt down the villages through which it had passed. As soon as they had entered the town of Louvain the Germans requisitioned food and lodging for their troops. They went to all the banks of the town, and took possession of the cash in hand. German soldiers burst open the doors of houses which had been abandoned by their inhabitants, pillaged them, and committed other excesses.

The German authorities took as hostages the Mayor of the city, Senator Van der Kelen, the Vice-Rector of the Catholic University, and the senior priest of the city, besides certain magistrates and aldermen. All the weapons possessed by the inhabitants, even fencing swords, had already been given up to the municipal authorities, and placed by them in the church of Saint Pierre.

GIRL RAPED

In a neighboring village, Corbeck-Loo, on Wednesday, August 19th, a young woman, aged twenty-two, whose husband was with the army, and some of her relations were surprised by a band of German soldiers. The persons who were with her were locked up in a deserted house, while she herself was dragged into another cottage, where she was raped by five soldiers successively. In the same village, on Thursday, August 20th, German soldiers fetched from their house a young girl, about sixteen years old, and her parents. They conducted them to a small deserted country house, and while some of them held back the father and mother, others entered the house, and, finding the cellar open, forced the girl to drink. They then brought her on to the lawn in front of the house, and raped her successively. Finally, they stabbed her in the breast with their bayonets. When this young girl had been abandoned by them after these abominable deeds, she was brought back to her parents' house, and the following day, in view of the gravity of her condition, she received extreme unction from the parish priest, and was taken to the hospital of Louvain, as her life was despaired of.

On August 24th and 25th Belgian troops made a sortie from the entrenched camp of Antwerp, and attacked the German army before Malines. The Germans were thrown back on Louvain and Vilvorde. On entering the villages which had been occupied by the enemy, the Belgian army found them devastated. The Germans, as they retired, had pillaged and burnt the villages, taking with them the male inhabitants, whom they forced to march in front of them. Belgian soldiers entering Hofstade, on August 25th, found the body of an old woman, who had been killed by bayonet thrusts. She still held in her hand the needle with which she was sewing when she was killed. A woman and her fifteen- or sixteen-year-old son lay on the ground, pierced by bayonets. A man had been hanged.

WORSE THAN THE TORTURES OF THE INQUISITION. ROASTING VICTIMS

At Sempst, a neighboring village, were found the bodies of two men, partially carbonized. One of them had his legs cut off at the knees; the other had the arms and legs cut off. A workman, whose burnt body has been seen by several witnesses, had been struck several times with bayonets, and then, while still alive the Germans had poured petroleum over him, and thrown him into a house to which they set fire. A woman who came out of her house was killed in the same way. A witness, whose evidence has been taken by a reliable British subject, declares that he saw on August 26th, not far from Malines, during the last Belgian attack, an old man tied by the arms to one of the rafters in the ceiling of his farm. The body was completely carbonized, but the head, arms and feet were unburnt. Further on, a child of about fifteen was tied up, the hands behind the back, and the body was completely torn open with bayonet wounds. Numerous corpses of peasants lay on the ground in positions of supplication, their arms lifted and their hands clasped.

The Belgian Consul in Uganda, who is now a volunteer in the Belgian army, reports that wherever the Germans passed the country has been devastated. The few inhabitants who remain in the villages tell of the atrocities committed by the enemy. Thus, at Wackerzeel, seven Germans are said to have successively violated a woman, and then to have killed her. In the same village they stripped a young boy to the waist, threatened him with death, holding a revolver to his chest, pricked him with lances, and then chased him into a field and shot at him, without, however, hitting him. Everywhere there is ruin and devastation. At Buecken many inhabitants were killed, including the priest, who was over eighty years old.

Between Impde and Wolverthem, two wounded Belgian soldiers lay near a house which was on fire. The Germans threw these two unfortunate men into the flames. At nightfall on August 26th, the German troops, repulsed by our soldiers, entered Louvain panic-stricken. Several witnesses affirm that the German garrison which occupied Louvain was erroneously informed that the enemy were entering the town. Men of the garrison immediately marched to the station, shooting haphazard the while, and there met the German troops who had been repulsed by the Belgians, the latter having just ceased the pursuit.

THE SACK OF LOUVAIN

Everything tends to prove that the German regiments fired on one another. At once, the Germans began bombarding the town, pretending that civilians had fired on the troops, a suggestion which is contradicted by all the witnesses, and could scarcely have been possible, because the inhabitants of Louvain had had to give up their arms to the municipal authorities several days before. The bombardment lasted till about ten o'clock at night. The

Germans then set fire to the town. Wherever the fire had not spread, the German soldiers entered the houses and threw fire grenades, with which some of them seem to be provided. The greater part of the town of Louvain was thus a prey to the flames, particularly the quarters of the upper town, comprising the modern buildings, the ancient cathedral of St. Pierre, the University buildings, together with the University Library, its manuscripts and collections, and the Municipal Theater.

The Commission considers it its duty to insist, in the midst of all these horrors, on the crime committed against civilization by the deliberate destruction of an academic library, which was one of the treasures of Europe.

The corpses of many civilians encumbered the streets and squares. On the road from Tirlemont to Louvain alone a witness counted more than fifty. On the doorsteps of houses could be seen carbonized bodies of inhabitants, who, hiding in their cellars, were driven out by the fire, tried to escape, and fell into the flames. The suburbs of Louvain suffered the same fate. We can affirm that the houses in all the districts between Louvain and Malines, and most of the suburbs of Louvain itself, have practically been destroyed.

A REFINEMENT OF TORTURE

On Wednesday morning, August 26th, the Germans brought to the station squares of Louvain a group of more than seventy-five persons, including several prominent citizens of the town, amongst whom were Father Coloboet and another Spanish priest, and also an American priest. The men were brutally separated from their wives and children, and, after having been subjected to the most abominable treatment by the Germans, who several times threatened to shoot them, they were forced to march to the village of Campenhout in front of the German troops. They were shut up in the village church, where they passed the night. About four o'clock the next morning a German officer told them they had better go to confessional, as they would be shot half an hour later. About half-past four they were liberated. Shortly afterwards they were again arrested by a German brigade, which forced them to march before them in the direction of Malines. In reply to a question of one of the prisoners, a German officer said they were going to give them a taste of the Belgian quickfirers before Antwerp. They were at last released on the Thursday afternoon at the gates of Malines.

THE BURNT WHITE FLAG

It appears from other witnesses that several thousand male inhabitants of Louvain who had escaped the shooting and the fire were sent to Germany for a purpose which is still unknown to us.

The fire at Louvain burnt for several days. An eye-witness, who left Louvain on August 30th, gave the following description of the town at that time: "Leaving Weert St. George's," he says, "I only saw burnt-down villages and half-crazy peasants, who, on meeting anyone, held up their hands as a sign of submission. Before every house, even those burnt down, hung a white flag, and the burnt rags of them could be seen among the ruins. At Weert St. George's I questioned the inhabitants on the causes of the German reprisals, and they affirmed most positively that no inhabitant had fired a shot, that in any case the arms had been previously collected, but that the Germans had taken vengeance on the population because a Belgian soldier belonging to the gendarmerie had killed an Uhlan."

CONTINUED INCENDIARISM AT LOUVAIN

"The population still remaining in Louvain have taken refuge in the suburb of Heverle, where they are extremely crowded. They have been cleared out of the town by the troops and the fire. The fire started a little beyond the American College, and the town is entirely destroyed, except for the Town Hall and the station. Furthermore, the fire was still burning to-day, and the Germans, far from taking any steps to stop it, seemed to feed it with straw, an instance of which I observed in the street adjoining the Town Hall. The cathedral and the theater are destroyed and have fallen in, as also the library; in short, the town has the appearance of an ancient ruined city, in the midst of which only a few drunken soldiers move about, carrying bottles of wine and liqueurs, while the officers themselves, seated in arm-chairs round the tables, drink like their men. In the streets the swollen bodies of dead horses rot in the sun, and the smell of fire and putrefaction pervades the whole place."

HOW THE GERMANS RUN AMOK IN A COUNTRY THEY INVADE

The Commission has not yet been able to obtain information about the fate of the Mayor of Louvain and of the other notables who were taken as hostages. The Commission is able to draw the following conclusions from the facts which have so far been brought to its notice:

In this war the occupation of any place is systematically accompanied and followed—sometimes even preceded—by acts of violence towards the civil population, which acts are contrary both to the usages of war and to the most elementary principles of humanity.

The German procedure is everywhere the same. They advance along a road, shooting inoffensive passers-by, particularly bi-cyclists, as well as peasants working in the fields.

In the towns or villages where they stop they begin by requisitioning food and drink, which they consume till intoxicated.

Sometimes, from the interior of deserted houses, they let off their rifles at random, and declare that it was the inhabitants who fired. Then the scenes of fire, murder, and especially pillage, begin, accompanied by acts of deliberate cruelty, without respect to sex or age. Even where they pretend to know the actual person guilty of the acts they allege they do not content them-selves with executing him summarily, but they seize the opportunity to decimate the population, pillage the houses, and then set them on fire.

After a preliminary attack and massacre they shut up the men in the church, and then order the women to return to their houses, and to leave their doors open all night.

SCREENS OF CIVILIANS IN ACTION. ABUSE OF THE WHITE FLAG AND THE RED CROSS

From several places the male population has been sent to Germany, there to be forced, it appears, to work at the harvest, as in the old days of slavery. There are many cases of the inhabitants being forced to act as guides, and to dig trenches and entrenchments for the Germans. Numerous witnesses assert that during their marches, and even when attacking, the Germans place civilians—men and women—in their front ranks, in order to prevent our soldiers firing. The evidence of Belgian officers and soldiers shows that German detachments do not hesitate to display either the white flag or the Red Cross flag, in order to approach our troops with impunity.

On the other hand, they fire on our ambulances and maltreat the ambulance men. They maltreat, and even kill, the wounded. The clergy seem to be particularly chosen as subjects for their brutality. Finally, we have in our possession expanding bullets, which had been abandoned by the enemy at Werchter, and we possess doctors' certificates showing that wounds must have been inflicted by bullets of this kind.

The documents and evidence on which these conclusions rest will be published in due course.

> The President,
>> (Signed) COOREMAN.
> The Members of the Commission,
>> (Signed) COUNT GOBLET D'ALVIELLA.
>>> RYCKMANS.
>>> STRAUSS.
>>> VAN CUTSEM.
> The Secretaries,
>> (Signed) CHEVALIER ERNST DE
>>> BUNSWYCK. ORTS.

Statement issued by Official Press Bureau, August 30th, 1914:

"The assumption of the German commander was, under the circumstances, so wide of probability, that it can only be supposed that, in the desire to conceal the facts, the first idea which occurred to him was seized upon as an excuse for an act without parallel in the history of civilized peoples.

"Louvain, a town of 45,000 people, a seat of learning, famous for its ancient and beautiful churches, and other buildings, many of them dating from the fifteenth century, has been utterly destroyed by one of the Kaiser's commanders, in a moment of passion, to cover a blunder of his own men.

"A town which in the Middle Ages was the capital of Brabant; a University founded in 1426, and ranked in the sixteenth century as the first in Europe; an Hôtel de Ville dating from 1448, one of the most beautiful examples of late Gothic architecture;

several churches of about the same date, to name one only, St. Pierre, with its wonderful stained glass windows, its beautiful tabernacle, and its richly carved organ, dating from 1556—all these have gone to revenge a fancied offense against the troops of the Kaiser.

"Only yesterday it was announced that the Emperor William had stated that 'the only means of preventing surprise attacks from the civil population has been to interfere with unrelenting severity and to create examples which by their frightfulness would be a warning to the whole country.' The case of Louvain is such an 'interference,' without even the miserable excuse suggested.

"Louvain is miles from the scene of real fighting. In international law it is recognized that 'the only legitimate end which the States would aim at in war is the weakening of the military forces of the enemy,' and the rules under the annex to Convention IV. of 1907, which expanded and amended the provisions of the Declaration of Brussels, lay down 'any destruction or seizure of enemy property not imperatively called for by military necessities' as forbidden.

"In destroying the ancient town of Louvain the German troops have committed a crime for which there can be no atonement, and humanity has suffered a loss which can never be repaired."

MURDERS AT DINANT

The _Daily Mail_, September 8th, 1914:

"Ostend, Monday.

"The Germans in a few hours by shell-fire and incendiarism have destroyed Dinant-sur-Meuse.

"The women were confined in convents, while hundreds of men were shot.

"A hundred prominent citizens were shot in the Place d'Armes.

"M. Hummers, the manager of a large weaving factory employing two thousand men, and M. Poncelet, the son of a former senator, were both shot, the latter in the presence of his six children.

"The Germans appeared at the branch of the National Bank, where they demanded all the cash in the safe. When M. Wasbeize, the manager, refused to give them the money they tried to blow the safe open. Not succeeding in this, they demanded the combination for the lock. The manager refused, whereupon the Germans shot him immediately, together with his two sons.

"The Prussians assert that these excesses have been committed because shots had been fired, though admittedly without result, from the heights overlooking Dinant."—*Reuter*.

MURDERS AT AERSCHOT

The Times, August 26th, 1914:

"They then compelled the inhabitants to leave their houses and marched them to a place two hundred yards from the town. There, without more ado, they shot M. Thielemans, the Burgomaster, his fifteen-year-old son, the clerk of the local judicial board, and ten prominent citizens. They then set fire to the town and destroyed it."

From the Belgian Minister's statement
"Murder of the Mayor of Aerschot."

DESTRUCTION AT TERMONDE

The *Daily Telegraph*, September 20th, 1914:

"On Wednesday, accompanied by M. Braun, I made a successful attempt to enter Termonde under most dangerous conditions. In some parts the streets were occupied by German soldiers. What a sight met our eyes! The Termonde I had known under circumstances so different—a quiet, pretty market town—now little more than a huge heap of blackened ruins. The Grande Place, with the exception of the Hôtel de Ville, on the roof of which the German flag hung limply, as though it were ashamed to float over the desolate scene, was in ruins. The hotel at which I had so often dined was reduced to a mass of débris. Termonde, indeed, was a city of desolation, caused by the devastating German hordes of savages. Here I obtained full proof of the statement of M. Thibbaut, regarding the treatment of women and the horrible debaucheries of the invaders. The scene at Termonde and the knowledge of what had happened there were enough to rouse every Christian to a determination to see that a nation capable of such enormities shall be wiped out forever."

JUSTIFICATION IN THE LEADING GERMAN
NEWSPAPERS

The Times, August 31st, 1914:

From *The Times* correspondent at Copenhagen, August 28th.

"The *Vossiche Zeitung's* account of the destruction of Louvain as a punishment for an alleged organized attack by the inhabitants on the German troops is characteristically cold-blooded. 'The art treasures of the old town exist no more.' Lovers of art will grieve, it continues, but there was no other way of punishing this population, whose devilish women poured boiling oil over the German troops.

"The *Lokalanzeiger* says the world will realize that the blame rests with the half-civilized population."

FOREWORD TO CHAPTER VII

The Right Honorable D. Lloyd George in his speech to the Welsh at the Queen's Hall, September 19th, 1914:

The world owes much to little nations (cheers) and to little men. (Laughter and cheers.) This theory of bigness—you must have a big empire and a big nation and a big man—well, long legs have their advantage in a retreat. (Laughter.) Frederick the Great chose his warriors for their height, and that tradition has become a policy in Germany. Germany applies that ideal to nations. She will allow only six-feet-two nations to stand in the ranks. But all the world owes much to the little five-feet-high nations. (Cheers.) The greatest art of the world was the work of little nations. The most enduring literature of the world came from little nations. The greatest literature of England came from her when she was a nation of the size of Belgium fighting a great empire. The heroic deeds that thrill humanity through generations were the deeds of little nations fighting for their freedom. Ah, yes, and the salvation of mankind came through a little nation. God has chosen little nations as the vessels by which he carries the choicest wines to the lips of humanity, to rejoice their hearts, to exalt their vision, to stimulate and to strengthen their faith, and if we had stood by when two little nations were being crushed and broken by the brutal hands of barbarism our shame would have rung down the everlasting ages. (Cheers.)

But Germany insists that this is an attack by a low civilization upon a higher. Well, as a matter of fact the attack was begun by the civilization which calls itself the higher one. Now, I am no apologist for Russia. She has perpetrated deeds of which I have no doubt her best sons are ashamed. But what empire has not? And Germany is the last empire to point the finger of reproach at Russia. (Hear, hear.) But Russia has made sacrifices for freedom—great sacrifices. You remember the cry of Bulgaria when she was torn by the most insensate tyranny that Europe has ever seen. Who listened to the cry? The only answer of the higher civilization was that the liberty of Bulgarian peasants was not worth the life of a single Pomeranian soldier. But the rude barbarians of the north, they sent their sons by the thousands to die for Bulgarian freedom. (Cheers.)

CHAPTER VII

THE ATTITUDE OF GERMANY'S ENEMIES

GERMANY OVERRUN BY SPIES FOR YEARS PAST

IF Germany has been overrun by spies for years past, she cannot complain of it without recalling the old fable of the pot calling the kettle black, for the number of her own spies must be a serious strain on the recruiting for the army—unless, indeed, there is a secret law of the Deutsches Reich that when a man has passed the age at which he can serve in the Landsturm he should take his place in the noble army of spies. Her enemies can only wish that Germany should be so hard pressed that she should call up her spies to take their place in East Prussia. If Germany is overrun with spies, it is quite certain that they must nearly all be Russians. The French and English supply of linguists is too limited.

On the other hand, the whole of Europe, especially England, is overrun with this lowest division of the Kaiser's army.

It goes without saying, that in time of war the respective participants seek to gain for themselves every possible advantage, including, as not the least of the advantages, that of having public opinion on their side. It is equally understandable that governments, for political or military reasons, often endeavor to conceal their real intentions until the decisive moment. In this matter, however, as in the conduct of war itself, there exists the basic principle, acknowledged throughout the civilized world, that no methods may be employed which could not be employed by men of honor even when they are opponents.

The pot pursues its task of blackening the kettle. The writer of this book hints that people at war have to try and win public opinion to their side, and that their Governments are sometimes obliged to conceal their real intentions till the last moment, but that there is a " basic principle, acknowledged throughout the civilized world, that no methods may be employed which could not be employed by men of honor even when they are opponents." This is too bad; it is like throwing mud at von Bernhardi. Besides, it is like telling some of the highest-placed personages at Potsdam that they are no gentlemen. Prince Lichnowsky is in the Kaiser's black books because his second telegram, saying that England had not promised to keep France neutral if Germany went to war with Russia, but only if Austria went to war with Russia, by herself, was suppressed in the German Foreign Office. The late General Grierson was the victim of a similar piece of treachery.

Letter from "A Gunner," friend and brother-officer of the late Sir James Grierson, reporting conversation with him, in *The Times*, August 26th, 1914:

"I asked him why he did not stay out his full time at Berlin when military attaché. He said: 'Because I simply could not stand any more of it. The place is a perfect hotbed of intrigue.' 'What sort of a man is the Kaiser himself?' I inquired. 'Oh,' he said, 'he is all right. He's a gentleman. But those around him are perfectly poisonous. This is the sort of thing they do. One day the Emperor suddenly said to me: "I am told, Colonel Grierson, but I need hardly say that I don't for one moment believe it, that you have given away to the French all the secrets of our Q. F. Artillery. Now I wish you would find out where that statement comes from, and put it in the form of an official report, and send it in to me through the War Office, saying that you do so by my special personal request." In less than a week,' Sir James continued, 'I found that it originated with ——, exactly as I expected it had, and so I duly sent it in as requested. Shortly afterwards I went on leave for about a month, and when I returned, the first thing the Emperor said to me was: "Oh, Colonel Grierson, you never sent me in that report I asked you for about our Q. F. Artillery." "I beg Your Majesty's pardon," I said, "but I sent it in in less than a week after you asked for it." "Well," said the Kaiser, "I have never received it. But I will inquire about it." Sure enough, the very next morning,' said the General, 'a whole row of them were down at my place, headed —— by himself, making most profuse apologies for the unfortunate oversight by which my report had been delayed, etc.'"

One cannot, unfortunately, acquit Russia of the charge of employing improper politics against Germany. It must, unfortunately, be said that even the Czar himself did not, at the breaking out of hostilities against Germany, show himself the gentleman upon a throne which he had formerly been believed by everyone to be.

The Russian Emperor addressed himself to Kaiser William in moving and friendly expressions, in which, pledging his solemn word and appealing to the grace of God, he besought the Kaiser, shortly before the outbreak of the war, to intervene at Vienna. There exists between Austria-Hungary and Germany an ancient and firm alliance which makes it the duty of both governments to offer unconditional support to each other in the moment that either one's vital interests come into question. There can be no doubt that the existence of Austria-Hungary is threatened by the Servian agitation. Despite this, the German Emperor, in offering his final counsels respecting the treatment of Servia and the concessions to be made to Russia, went, in his desire for peace, almost to the point where Austria could have had doubts of Germany's fidelity to the obligations of the alliance.

The accusation that the Czar did not keep faith with Germany resolves itself into the Kaiser attributing his own insincerities to the Czar.

Undoubtedly the Czar did in the most solemn manner appeal to the Kaiser to intervene at Vienna, to prevent Austria proceeding to extremities with Servia before the great Powers had done their best to straighten out the question. Undoubtedly there is the closest alliance between Germany and Austria to support each other unconditionally when any vital interest of either is in question. Allow that the existence of Austria-Hungary was threatened by Servian agitation, though integrity is the proper word, the German

Emperor told England and Russia that he must leave his ally unfettered to form her own opinions; the writer of this volume of blandishments informs the guileless American that the German Emperor " in offering his final counsels respecting the treatment of Servia, and the concessions to be made to Russia, went in his desire for peace almost to the point where Austria could have had doubts of Germany's fidelity." Austria had the best possible reason for doubting its fidelity, having sent the ultimatum to Servia at Germany's orders and insisted on an answer in forty-eight hours, to demands so outrageous that there was practically no chance of the war not happening.

In a remarkable letter to " The Times," of September 22nd, Mr. W. Llewellyn Williams, puts the whole matter in a nutshell. " Inter alia " he says:

"It almost looks as if the Kaiser had hoped to play the same *rôle* again in July, 1914 (as in 1909). The White Paper contains ample evidence (see, *e.g.*, Nos. 32, 47, and 71) that both Germany and Austria believed that the Powers of the Triple Entente were not prepared to go to war with Servia. The precipitancy of Germany, therefore, in sending the ultimatum to Russia on July 30th, at a time when Austria had not 'banged the door,' may be explainable on the supposition that she wanted to score another diplomatic triumph on her own account and share none of it with her ally."

He then proceeds to prove the guilt of Austria with damning terseness:

"On July 20th the Russian Ambassador, anticipating no crisis, left Vienna on a fortnight's leave of absence. No sooner was his back turned than Austria, on July 23rd, delivered her ultimatum to Servia. The ultimatum was accompanied by a forty-eight-hours' time-limit. Before, therefore, the Russian Ambassador could return to Vienna it was probable that the time-limit would have expired.

"On the very day when the ultimatum was delivered at Belgrade the French Ambassador called on Count Berchtold, and (says Sir M. de Bunsen) 'was not even informed that the Note was at that very moment being presented at Belgrade.' Nor was this all. At the moment when he was keeping the French Ambassador in the dark, Count Berchtold knew that the President of the French Republic and the President of the French Council could not 'reach France, on their return from Russia, for four or five days.' (Sir G. Buchanan's dispatch, dated July 24th.)

"Sir Edward Grey saw that, if the situation was to be saved, the time-limit would have to be extended. For the reasons given, there were grave difficulties in the way of France and Russia intervening in time. Representations were therefore sought to be made in Berlin and Vienna. The Kaiser seems to have been away from home, and the German Foreign Minister was evidently not in the confidence of his Imperial master, and knew no more than the rest of the world of the Austrian ultimatum. (Sir H. Rumbold's dispatch, July 25th.) Worse than all, Count Berchtold, the Austrian Foreign Secretary, who should have been at his post in Vienna during those anxious forty-eight hours when the sands were running out, was away at Ischl on July 25th, and could not be approached. (Sir H. Rumbold, July 25th.)

"Comment is unnecessary. On July 24th Sir G. Buchanan, writing to Sir E. Grey, said:

"'It looks as though Austria purposely chose this moment to present their ultimatum.'

"Is it not clear that Sir G. Buchanan's suspicion was well-founded, and that Austria and Germany conspired together to place an intolerable affront on the Powers of the Triple Entente, and hoped by the low cunning which is sometimes dignified by the name of 'diplomacy' to do so with the impunity which they enjoyed in 1909?"

Nevertheless, Russia at this very time not only continued its mobilization against Austria, but

also simultaneously brought its troops into a state
of preparedness for war against Germany. It is
impossible that this could have been done without
the order of the Czar. The conduct of the Russian
Minister of Foreign Affairs, of the Chief of the
General Staff, and of the War Minister was of a
piece with this attitude of the ruler. They assured the German Ambassador and the German
military attaché upon their word of honor that
troops were not being mobilized against Germany
and that no attack upon Germany was planned.
The fact, however, proved that the decision to
make war upon Germany had already been reached
at that time.

The reason which impelled the Czar and his
chief advisers to employ such base tactics with
the help of their word of honor and appeals to
the Supreme Being is plain. Russia requires a
longer time for mobilization than Germany. In
order to offset this advantage, to deceive Germany,
and to win a few days' start, the Russian Government stooped to a course of conduct as to which
there can be but one judgment among brave and
upright opponents. No one knew better than
the Czar the German Emperor's love of peace.
This love of peace was reckoned upon in the whole
despicable game. Fortunately the plan was perceived on the German side at the right time.
Advices received by Germany's representative
in St. Petersburg concerning the actual Russian
mobilization against Germany moved him to add

to the report given upon the Russian word of honor a statement of his own conviction that an attempt was obviously being made to deceive him. We find also that the character of the Russian operations had been rightly comprehended by so unimpeachable an organ as the English *Daily Graphic* of August 1st which said: "If the mobilization order is also carried through in the provinces bordering on Germany, the work of the preservers of peace is ended, for Germany will be compelled to answer with the mobilization of her armed forces. We confess that we are unable to understand this attitude of Russia in connection with the renewal of the negotiations with Austria."

Germany, who had all along pooh-poohed the capacity of Russia to make an army which could match her own, suddenly became aware, in the spring of 1914, that within a couple of years Russia would have three to five millions more soldiers than Germany, and of excellent quality, that her field-artillery was already magnificent, and that by 1916 she would have a huge supply of a new siege-gun, which would superannuate any fortress. If Germany was to have the hegemony of Europe, for which she had been plotting and arming since 1870, France must be smashed at once, and Russia scotched before she became invincible. A war could be forced over Servia, and if Russia would by any chance submit to another humiliation like that of 1909 (the Bosnia-Herzegovina seizure), Servia and Greece could be smashed up, to rob Russia of her prestige and future allies. The subjugation of Servia was to be followed by the seizure of Salonika. Germany was practically ready for war; Russia had few railways, and many of her forces were at vast distances, as it was believed.

It soon became clear that Russia considered the integrity of Servia vital, and might be put into the scales with Austria. England, France, and the third member of the Triple Alliance, Italy, were sincerely anxious for peace. They imagined that the German Emperor would be as anxious, because he had striven so hard to keep the peace of Europe during the Balkan War. They did not know that the Balkan Wars had disappointed his calculations—that he would have been at a disadvantage if the Triple Alliance had had to fight against the Triple Entente with his existing artillery, and with the Balkan League on the side of Russia.

He would not join the three Western Powers in making representations to Austria; he represented that he could do nothing, whereas, since Austria was merely acting as his catspaw, the one word "stop" would have been sufficient. He could have stopped it by holding up his little finger. He sent disingenuous telegrams to the Czar and King George. He told the Western Powers that the Austrian Ambassador was having perfectly friendly conversations with the Russian Foreign Office, and he went on making his preparations for war with feverish haste, without formally mobilizing, having already, on the day that Austria's ultimatum expired, commenced wrecking the Stock Exchange of London and the

Paris Bourse (to which he had thoughtfully
devoted the sums of four millions and two
millions respectively), so that England and France
might be too paralyzed financially to move. He
knew that all the other Stock Exchanges except
those which had been forewarned, would follow.

The Czar, a simple, straightforward, God-
fearing man, not easily moved, then took up the
attitude which "Truth about Germany" de-
nounces as unworthy of a gentleman upon a
throne. He saw that Austria did not mean business unless the penalty was war, so he mobilized
his army corps on the Austrian frontier. Germany felt cruelly injured by such behavior, and
grew so restive that the Czar mobilized the army
corps on her frontier also. Then came the double
ultimatum. Russia was asked to give an undertaking within twelve hours that she would de-
mobilize, and France was asked to reply within
eighteen hours if war with Russia meant war with
her. Russia in a bored and dignified way declined
to give any answer. France said that she would
do what suited her. And Germany declared war.

It should be added in fairness to Russia that,
after she had begun to mobilize, she was as
sincerely desirous of peace as ever. She mobilized because she saw that she could not preserve
peace with honor without mobilizing. She
would either have had to fight unprepared or to
accept another humiliation.

It is customary among civilized nations that a
formal declaration of war shall precede the beginning of hostilities, and all powers, with the excep-

tion of some unimportant scattered states, have obligated themselves under international law to observe this custom. Neither Russia nor France has observed this obligation. Without a declaration of war, Russian troops crossed the German border, opened fire on German troops, and attempted to dynamite bridges and buildings. In like manner, without a declaration of war, French aviators appeared above unfortified cities in South Germany, and sought, by throwing bombs, to destroy the railways. French detachments crossed the German border and occupied German villages. French aviators flew across neutral Holland and the then neutral Belgium to carry out warlike plans against the lower Rhine district of Germany. A considerable number of French officers, disguised in German uniforms, tried to cross the Dutch-German frontier in an automobile in order to destroy institutions in German territory.

In this paragraph the Germans accurately describe their own violations of French and Russian territory and divide them impartially between the Russians and the French. Attempting surprises in uniforms taken from the dead or from prisoners is a specialty in German tactics. By this means and by bringing up quick-firing guns in Red Cross wagons and by a judicious abuse of the white flag (see page 134), they have treacherously inflicted much damage on a generous and sporting enemy. Whatever either side did before the formal declaration of war, no

> important results were achieved. The French certainly cannot be accused of invading Germany before the declaration, because, to avoid collisions, they withdrew all their men ten kilometers from the frontier, except where there was any position to be held, and then they were kept in the position.

It is plain that both France and Russia desired to compel Germany to make the first step in declaring war, so that the appearance of having broken the peace might, in the eyes of the world, rest upon Germany. The Russian government even attempted to disseminate through a foreign news agency the report that Germany had declared war on Russia, and it refused, contrary to the usage among civilized nations, to permit to be telegraphed the report of the German Ambassador that Russia had rejected the final German note concerning war and peace.

> This is exactly on a par with the German refusal of the British Ambassador's telegram under similar circumstances.

Germany, for its part, in the hope that peace might yet be maintained, subjected itself to the great disadvantage of delaying its mobilization in the first decisive days in the face of the measures of its probable enemy. When, however, the German Emperor realized that peace was no longer possible, he declared war against France and Russia honorably, before the beginning of hostilities, thus bringing into contrast the moral courage to assume the responsibility for the beginning of the conflict as against the moral cowardice of both opponents, whose fear of public opinion was such that they did not dare openly to admit their intentions to attack Germany.

> Far from France and Russia desiring to compel Germany to make the first step, so that the blame of breaking the peace might rest on Germany, they did not desire to have war at all. But Germany declared war because she had made up her mind to do so unless she obtained what she wanted. Russia's refusal to allow the report of the German Ambassador to be telegraphed was a purely technical grievance.
>
> As Germany was ready for war before she allowed the crisis to commence, she could allow the enemy to mobilize without injuring herself. I cannot understand why the writer of this book makes such a fal-lal about Germany having the courage to declare war against France and Russia honorably, while they lacked the moral courage to take the responsibility of beginning and maneuvered for the blame of it to fall upon her. The book attributes it to their fear of public opinion, a likely enough reason if they were trying to maneuver her into making a declaration. But why should they? It was clear enough that the war was her doing. England, the most pacific of them all, was the only country to declare war.

Germany, moreover, cared in a humane and proper manner at the outbreak of the war for

those non-combatant subjects of hostile states—
traveling salesmen, travelers for pleasure, patients
in health resorts, etc.—who happened to be in the
country at the time. In isolated cases, where
the excitement of the public grew disquieting,
the authorities immediately intervened to protect
persons menaced. In Russia, however, in France,
and especially in Belgium the opposite of decency
and humanity prevailed. Instead of referring
feelings of national antipathy and of national
conflicting interests to the decision of the battle-
field, the French mishandled in the most brutal
manner the German population and German
travelers in Paris and other cities, who neither
could nor wished to defend themselves, and who
desired solely to leave the hostile country at once.
The mob threatened and mishandled Germans in
the streets, in the railway stations, and in the
trains, and the authorities permitted it.

**However the Germans may have behaved to
the ordinary non-combatant subjects of hostile
states, such as commercial travelers, tourists, and
invalids, it is certain that they behaved much
worse to Ambassadors and Consuls than their
opponents. Reuter's telegram to " The Times "
about the departure of the Russian Ambassador
is an example, and a foreign Consul at Danzig
has yet worse to tell; and official reports show
that the ill-treatment of Russians in Germany
was quite as bad as anything done to Germans
anywhere.**

The occurrences in Belgium are infamous beyond all description. Germany would have exposed itself to the danger of a military defeat if it had still respected the neutrality of Belgium after it had been announced that strong French detachments stood ready to march through that country against the advancing German army. The Belgian Government was assured that its interests would be conscientiously guarded if it would permit the German army to march through its territory. In answer to this assurance was a declaration of war. In making this declaration it acted perhaps not wisely, but unquestionably within its formal rights. It was, however, not right, but, on the contrary, a disgraceful breach of right, that the eyes of wounded German soldiers in Belgium were gouged out, and their ears and noses cut off; that surgeons and persons carrying the wounded were shot at from houses.

It is frankly impossible to understand what the writer meant this paragraph to prove. What was infamous?—that there were strong French detachments ready to march through the country against the Germans may be disproved by the fact that when the Germans had violated Belgian territory and the Belgians needed and besought the help of France as soon as ever they could get it, there were few French troops ready to advance into Belgium, and the French had no plans whatever for utilizing Belgian defenses to delay the German advances.

The assurances to Belgium that all her interests would be "conscientiously guarded" if she would break her treaty and allow the German army to pass through Belgium—offered by one of the Powers which had guaranteed her treaty—may be characterized as one of the most blackguardly political suggestions in history.

The alleged outrages on the wounded and the doctors are German outrages attributed to Belgians.

Private dwellings of Germans in Antwerp were plundered, German women were dragged naked through the streets by the mob and shot to death before the eyes of the police and the militia. Captains of captured German ships in Antwerp were told that the authorities could not guarantee their lives. German tourists were robbed of their baggage, insulted, and mishandled, sick persons were driven from the German hospital, children were thrown from the windows of German homes into the streets and their limbs were broken. Trustworthy reports of all these occurrences, from respectable and responsible men, are at hand. We perceive with the deepest indignation that the cruelties of the Congo have been outdone by the motherland. When it comes to pass that in time of war among nations the laws of humanity respecting the helpless and the unarmed, the women and children, are no longer observed, the world is reverting to barbarism.

The Germans are here attributing to the Belgians in Antwerp the ordinary German procedure.

Even in war times, humanity and honor should still remain the distinguishing marks of civilization.

The English believed that "even in war times, humanity and honor " would have received more consideration from the people who talked so much about culture and their civilizing mission.

That French and Russians, in their endeavors to spy upon Germany and destroy her institutions, should disguise themselves in German uniforms is a sorry testimony to the sense of honor possessed by our opponents. He who ventures to conduct espionage in a hostile land or secretly to plant bombs, realizes that he risks the penalty of death, whether he be a civilian or a member of the army. Up to the present, however, it has not been customary to use a uniform, which should be respected even by the enemy, to lessen the personal risk of the spy and to facilitate his undertaking.

It is inconceivable that the great Germans who allowed their name to be attached to this book could have seen its contents. The whole history of the war teems with the treacherous use of the uniforms of their enemies by Germans—officers as well as privates. At its very opening a motorload of Germans disguised as English officers made a dash into Liége to capture or kill General Leman, and the Hon. Archer Windsor–Clive,

The Real Truth About Germany

the well-known cricketer, who has died of his wounds, was shot at close quarters by a German officer dressed in an English military cloak whom he was in the act of saluting. The writer of the paragraph probably meant to delude Americans with academical condemnations.

For a number of years there have been increasing indications that France, Russia, and England were systematically spying upon the military institutions of Germany. In the eight years from 1906 to 1913, 113 persons were found guilty of attempted or accomplished espionage of a grave nature. The methods employed by these spies included theft, attacks upon military posts, and the employment of German officers' uniforms as disguises. The court proceedings threw a clear light upon the organization and operations of espionage in Germany. This espionage was directed from central points in foreign countries, often in the small neighboring neutral states. Repeatedly it appeared that the foreign embassies and consulates in Germany assisted in this work; it was also discovered that Russia, France, and England were exchanging reports which they had received concerning Germany's means of defense.

It is to be understood from this paragraph that Germany totally disapproves of the use of spies, and has never had any in her employ. In Germany itself, in eight years only, one hundred and thirteen foreigners were found guilty of attempted

or accomplished espionage of a grave nature. Considering German methods, it may be taken for granted that at least a hundred of them were innocent. The offenses included theft, and attacks on military posts, and using German officers' uniforms as disguises. If one Englishman was caught in a German uniform during those eight years, he must have been quietly murdered, for it never came into the papers, which devoted volumes to the two officers who were caught and imprisoned for years on a discredited scoundrel's false accusation that they had been making observations of German coast defenses. What spies there were in Germany, for linguistic reasons, must have been Russians, or Germans in the pay of their enemies. These may have included a certain number of Alsatians and Lorrainers who wished to be French subjects. But they would be peculiarly liable to suspicion. On the other hand, foreign countries have swarmed with German spies, who, if they had been hunted out with German thoroughness, would have made an army corps.

This espionage system was supported with large funds. It endeavored whenever possible to seduce military persons and officials to betray their country, and, when this was not possible, it devoted its attention to doubtful characters of every sort. It began its work with petty requests of a harmless appearance, followed these with inducements to violations of duty, and then proceeded with threats of exposure to compel its victims to betray their country further. Exact instructions, complete in the minutest detail, were given to the spies for the carrying on of their work; they were equipped with photographic apparatus, with skeleton keys, forged passes, etc.; they received fixed monthly salaries, especial bonuses for valuable information, and high rewards for especially secret matters, such as army orders, descriptions of weapons, and plans of fortifications. Principal attention was paid to our boundaries, railroads, bridges, and important buildings on lines of traffic, which were spied upon by specially trained men. With the reports of these spies as their basis, our opponents have carefully planned the destruction of the important German lines of communication.

It is really very amusing to have the instructions, equipment, and " modus operandi " of the German spy system divulged to the world by the German authorities in the spirited sketch supplied by this paragraph of the machinations of foreign governments. That the net was a wide one we know from the instance of the Liverpool boy clerk, whose attention was drawn to the fact that his modest earnings could be supplemented by easy and well-paid employment. He wrote to the German Foreign Office, or something equally high-sounding, about it, and was given instructions which led to his examining the forts, chiefly shoddy affairs used for the training of Territorials round Liverpool. The German War Office complained that his reports were not of much technical value, and the liberal pay he received for them all told was two pounds, sent in English Postal Orders. This came out when he was tried and sentenced in a British law court a few months ago.

The extraordinary watchfulness of the German military officials immediately before the declaration of war and since then has been able to render futile the whole system of foreign attempts against our means of communication in every single instance, but a great number of such attempts have been made. All these things prove beyond doubt that a war against Germany has long been planned by our opponents.

The mention of the extraordinary watchfulness which rendered futile the whole system of foreign attempts against German means of communication just before the war—attempts of which ninety-nine per cent. could only have existed in German nerve attacks or the fiction in which their Official Press delights—is only an introduction to the statement that " all these things prove beyond doubt that the war against Germany has long been planned by our opponents."

11

FOREWORD TO CHAPTER VIII

LIES NAILED TO THE COUNTER

From *Daily Mail* correspondent:

"New York, Monday, September 7th.

"The Press of the United States to-day calmly and emphatically rejects the appeal for the sympathy of this nation made by the leading savants, authors, statesmen, financiers, and industrial magnates of Germany in the form of a book giving the Kaiser's case under the title "The Truth About Germany."

"In dealing with this appeal the *New York Times* observes: 'No voice or pen, however eloquent or gifted, can convince an impartial world of the justice of Germany's cause or change the rooted belief of right-thinking men that she is battling for ends that, if attained, would retard, rather than advance, the cause of civilization and make the peace, prosperity, and happiness of the nations less secure.

"'These men of Germany ask us to give no heed to the lies of their enemies. In this land of enlightenment public opinion does not take form on anybody's lies. We take no count of perversions sent out from London or Paris. We have sought truth in its undefiled sources in the British White Paper and in the memorandum of the German Foreign Office, in the observed and acknowledged policies of the combatant nations, and in the utterances of their men of authority. The princes and professors who pay us the compliment of this appeal to our candid judgment will not impeach the testimony of their Foreign Office.

"'If there was suspension of judgment in the first weeks of the war, all doubt vanished and full conviction came when the official documents and records were published. The American people there read of the untiring efforts of Sir Edward Grey to reach a peaceful adjustment through a conference of the Powers, of his appeals, to which France, Russia, and Italy gave an immediate assenting response and which Germany alone met with evasion, excuse, disfavor, and refusal.

"'From the German memorandum they learn that the Kaiser's Government had from the first sustained and encouraged Austria in a policy of war, and had denied the rights of any other Power to stand between her and the Servian objects of her wrath. It is wholly futile, it is an affront to our intelligence for these German suppliants for our favor to tell us now that Russia and England brought on the war, that Germany did not choose the path of blood, that the sword was forced into the hands of the German Emperor; nor can our favor or sympathy be won by misrepresenting the motives of England, France, and Russia.

"'In the face of Sir Edward Grey's labors for peace, why tell us that England "encouraged this war" because she was determined to check the commercial growth of Germany? Why tell us that the war was "provoked by Russia" because of an outrageous desire for revenge?

"'These German advocates talk as though we had just arrived from the moon. We are unmoved by their picture of the Slav peril. Why is it that Germany fears the Slav? England is not afraid; France has no fear; Italy, Belgium, and Holland are all undisturbed. We should like to see a satisfactory answer to the question why, when all the rest of Europe is calm, Germany stands in terror of the Slav?

"'The authors of this book make a wretched defense of Germany's crime against international morality and her invasion of neutral Belgium. "In our place the Government of the United States would not have acted differently." Speak for yourselves, gentlemen. Our recent repeal of a statute that was by a great part of our people deemed to be in conflict with one of our treaties speaks for us.'

"The article refers to the disgust with which the inhabitants of the United States listen to the Kaiser's 'blasphemous invocations to Divine favor upon his bloody enterprises' and concludes: 'These gentlemen of Germany plead in vain. We can give them no help. To quote their own words in a truer sense than their own, "The country of George Washington and Abraham Lincoln places itself upon the side of a just cause and one worthy of humanity's blessing."'"

CHAPTER VIII

LIES ABOUT GERMANY

THE MACHINATIONS OF ENGLAND AND FRANCE TO PUT GERMANY IN THE WRONG—LIES ON ALL SIDES.

GERMANY has now not only to battle against a world in arms but it must also defend itself against lies and slanders which have been piled up around it like a hostile rampart. There is no cable at our disposal. England has either cut the cables, or is in possession of them. No German description of what has actually occurred can be sent by telegraph; the wires are carrying into the world only the distortions of our enemies. Germany is shut off as with a hedge from the outside world, and the world is supplied solely with news given out by our enemies. This language is strictly true; for the boldest, nay, the most impudent imagination would be unable to invent anything to exceed the false and absurd reports already printed by foreign newspapers. In view of what we have experienced during this first week of the war, we can already calmly assert that when the editors of foreign newspapers come

later to compare their daily news of this week with
the actual occurrences as testified to by authentic
history they will all open their eyes in astonish-
ment and anger over all the lies which the countries
hostile to Germany have sent over the cables to
bamboozle the whole world.

This German complaint to America about lies
reminds me of the famous picture in the Vatican
of Alexander VI., the most wicked of all the
Popes, with his eyes fixed on a portrayal of the
Resurrection.   One would have thought it a
painful subject for him.   The Germans cannot
even be true to themselves, for while their ac-
credited Ambassador in Washington, " Count
John Bernstorff," has been giving to the United
States the correct version of everything that has
happened, this chapter in this book tells us on the
authority of Prince Bülow, Ex-Chancellor, Field-
Marshal von der Goltz, and the rest of them,
heads of all the greatest institutions in Germany,
that " no German description of what has actually occurred can be sent by telegraph. . . .
Germany is shut off as with a hedge from the
outside world."   Poor " Count John Bernstorff,"
lying so bravely! Has he found out yet that
Germany's National Committee has announced
to the civilized world that it is impossible for him
to have received any German description of what
has actually occurred?
One wonders how the committee dares to say
that " the most impudent imagination would be
unable to invent anything to exceed the false and

absurd reports already printed by foreign newspapers." The German official reports disseminated by their own wireless, beggar the ordinary newspaper imagination. They have reached such a pitch that even the newspapers of Holland—poor little Holland! which has to act as a sort of office for German communications with the outside world—has no newspaper which will print them. The Germans have had to start a Dutch newspaper of their own for the purpose.

GERMAN PAPER TO BE STARTED IN HOLLAND

From the *Globe:*

"The Hague, September 14th.

"A new paper, *De Toesdend*, which is financed in Germany, is now circulated at The Hague for the dissemination of German news in the Dutch language.

"The Dutch papers have refused to be influenced by German agents."—*Exchange Special.*

And the Press of the rest of the world, notably that of Italy, the sleeping partner in the Triple Alliance, and the United States, for which this feeding-bottle book was prepared, ladles derision on to the official German reports, which, if they serve any use at all, serve to keep the German public in the dark about what their Government does not wish them to know. Take, for instance, the statement that there are two hundred and twenty thousand French, English, Russian, and Belgian prisoners in Germany, not including the forty thousand prisoners captured in Maubeuge, or the statement issued just before the middle of September that the total German losses in the war amount to four thousand killed and under

twenty thousand wounded—this after a couple of
million men had been attacking in close formation
for two or three weeks; this after the carnage at
Lunéville, where the killed were estimated at
twenty-five thousand! The same official wireless
agency sent the news to Grand Canary, faithfully
recorded in its newspaper, which has arrived in
London, that at the battle of Heligoland the Germans lost five small cruisers, but the English
seven large battle-cruisers. These items deserve
mention in any list of war-lies.

It may be impossible to control newspapers,
even when you have a Hammann and a special
bureau for the purpose, devoted entirely to se-
curing that nothing which is not absolutely true
shall find its way into print. But the official
reports of War Offices stand on a different footing,
and until the German authorities imitate the
English and Russian authorities in issuing no
reports until they are absolutely certain of their
truth, in checking every attempt to exaggerate,
in chronicling disasters as faithfully as victories,
it is no good sending complaints to America of
lies about Germany. It is unkind of Munich to
have had riots demanding the truth from the
Government.

Much of all this has already become ridiculous;
we must laugh over it despite the solemnity of the
crisis in which we are living—for example, the
bestowal of the cross of the Legion of Honor upon
the city of Liége by the French President because
it victoriously repulsed the attack of the Germans.

Witness, too, the telegrams of congratulation sent by the King of England and the Czar of Russia to the Belgian King upon the victory of Liége! The joy over such "German defeats" will prove just as brief as the jubilation over such "Belgian victories." Such lies have short legs, and the truth will in any case soon overtake them.

> **Undoubtedly the confusion between Liége and its forts betrayed President Poincaré into a position which must have seemed supremely ridiculous to German eyes. But it was no funnier than the " Goeben " and the " Breslau " steaming out of Messina with bands playing and colors flying and protestations of death or victory when they were only going to run away to the Dardanelles and be sold like unredeemed pawnbrokers' pledges to the Turks. These things will happen unless you are as careful as the British Official Press Bureau.**

But there are other lies of a more serious character and of more dangerous import—all such as misrepresent Germany's attitude and defame German character. Such defamation is designed to disturb old friendships and transform them into bitter estrangement; such defamation can also attain its hostile purpose wherever people do not say daily to themselves: "It is an enemy that reports such things about Germany; let us be wise and suspend our judgment till we know actual results, till we know what is surely the truth."

There are two classes of Germans, one consisting of ordinary kindly human beings, concerned with the usual interests of civilized beings, and distinguished by ability in music, scholarship, science, or art, more frequently, perhaps, than individuals in other nations. The other class is concerned with Germany's mission to subdue the world by " hacking its way through "—the people to whom von Bernhardi's book is Gospel. This class lays Germany's attitude open to misrepresentation and her character to defamation, and a sufficiently strong indictment can be laid against her without either one or the other.

Let us select several facts as examples and as evidence—facts connected with the preparation for this war, as well as with the conduct of it thus far.

All the cables controlled by the English-French-Russian coalition disseminate the lie about the ostensibly "preventive war" that Germany wished and prepared for. The German "White Book" prints documents proving THE WHITE PURITY OF THE GERMAN CONSCIENCE as represented by Kaiser, Chancellor, and people. It reveals also the profound grief of the German Kaiser over the sly and insidious perfidy of the Czar, toward whom he steadily maintained German fidelity even in hours of grave danger. What Russia did was more than a mere attack, it was a treacherous assault. The following facts prove this: The German mobilization was ordered on

August 1st, whereas Russia began to mobilize fully four weeks earlier, or about the beginning of July. Papers found on several Russian harvest-laborers arrested in the district of Konitz show that the Russian military authorities had already by July 1st—*i. e.*, immediately after the tragedy at Sarajevo—sent to the leaders of these men mustering-in orders, which were to be distributed immediately after a further word should be given. These confiscated papers prove that Russia hoped to be able to mobilize against Austria before Germany could get official information of Russia's measures. The Russian authorities purposely avoided the usual course of sending these orders through the Russian consuls, and they assigned "military exercises" as the object of this call to the colors.

It is quite certain that Germany meant to go to war this summer, and made Austria send the ultimatum to Servia with that object. Mobilization papers to Germans in distant parts of the world prove this. If Russia did send mustering-in orders to her harvest-laborers in Germany on July 1st, it does not prove that any military measures were intended. It was merely a proper precaution growing out of the murder of the Archduke Francis Ferdinand, to get them out of a hostile country (where they were in large numbers) in case of trouble. To say that German mobilization was ordered on August 1st, whereas Russian mobilization began four weeks earlier,

is reversing the order of things. Germany was as good as mobilized before she inspired Austria to send the ultimatum, though her formal mobilization was not announced till the war was breaking out. Russia only mobilized when it became apparent that Germany and Austria meant to try and squeeze her. On July 31st British steamers were forcibly detained at Hamburg and not allowed to proceed after that day.

July 25th: Military exercises at Krasnoye-Selo were suddenly broken off, and the troops returned at once to their garrison. The maneuvers had been called off. The military cadets were advanced at once to officers instead of waiting, as usual, till autumn.

These two moves were in consequence of Austria's ultimatum to Servia, and there is no proof that the further word was given. It is interesting to find that these were military exercises: so the ostensible reason was probably the true one.

July 26th: All ships and boats are forbidden to sail in the waters between Helsingfors and Yorkkele; and navigation between Sweden and Finland is closed.

July 28th: Partial mobilization; 16 army corps to be increased to the strength of 32 corps. On the same day the Czar begs for friendly mediation, and on the same day the Russian Minister of

Foreign Affairs and the Russian Minister of War give the German military attaché, upon their own initiative, their solemn word of honor that no mobilization has taken place.

> July 26th: Considering the fondness the Germans have shown for mines, the precaution was not unnecessary. July 28th: There was no reason why the Czar should not have been quite honest in his desire for peace while he was taking a precaution against surprise from a nation whose von Bernhardis have always urged it to take every advantage it could to neutralize the superior strength of an enemy by "slimness." The German jingoes, when they drank "to the day" —meaning the day on which the German fleet was to meet the English—always meant to use every device they could to prevent it being a square stand-up fight between the two fleets. The English fleet was to be weakened first with every form of insidious attack. The Russian is no fool; he may be just as good as the German in avoiding the technical forms of mobilization while he secures most of its effects. And, after all, this quibbling about the technicalities of mobilization is not vital. It is a mere form of diplomacy. The vital point at issue among all these recriminations was: the sincerity of the desire for peace. Russia sincerely desired peace, but did not mean to be caught napping. Germany meant to slap Russia in the face if she would not fight. These two central facts make all the recriminations about mobilization superfluous.

July 30th: The second and third Russian cavalry divisions appear on the German frontier between Wirballen and Augustov. The Czar issues a ukase calling to the colors the reserves in 23 entire governments and in 80 districts of other governments; also the naval reserves in 64 districts, or 12 Russian and one Finnish government; also the Cossacks on furlough in a number of districts; also the necessary reserve officers, physicians, horses, and wagons.

July 31st: General mobilization of the whole Russian army and navy. The German steamer *Eitel Friedrich*, which keeps up a regular service between Stettin and St. Petersburg, is stopped by a Russian torpedo-boat and brought into Reval, where the crew were made prisoners. The Russians blow up the railway bridge on Austrian territory between Szozakowa and Granica.

July 30th and 31st: As the bellicose intentions of Germany became more and more obvious, the Czar made extensive preparations on the first of these two days, and ordered a general mobilization of his army and navy on the second. It was necessary to turn the tables on Germany, and let her know what Austria's persisting in her course meant. On July 31st the Czar sent the following telegram to the Emperor:

" I thank thee from my heart for the mediation, which leaves a gleam of hope that even now all may end peacefully. *It is technically impossible to discontinue our military operations,* which are

rendered necessary by Austria's mobilization. We are far from wishing for war, and so long as the negotiations with Austria regarding Servia continue, my troops will not undertake any provocative action. I give thee my word upon it. I trust with all my strength in God's grace, and I hope for the success of thy mediation in Vienna, and for the welfare of our countries and the peace of Europe.

"Thy most devoted,
"NICHOLAS."

The Czar makes no attempt here to conceal his military operations. It was indisputable that Austria had already given the orders to mobilize against Russia. The Kaiser replied with a long telegram, which ended up with a distinct threat.

"In answer to thy appeal to my friendship and thy prayer for my help I undertook mediatory action between the Austria-Hungarian Government and thine. While this action was in progress thy troops were mobilizing against my ally, Austria-Hungary, in consequence of which, as I have already informed thee, my mediation was rendered nearly illusory. Nevertheless, I have continued it.

"Now, however, I receive trustworthy news of your serious preparations for war even on my eastern frontier. The responsibility for the safety of my kingdom compels me to take definite retaliatory measures. My efforts to maintain the peace of the world have now reached their utmost possible limit.

"It will not be I who am responsible for the

calamity which threatens the whole civilized world. Even at this moment it lies in thy power to avert it. Nobody threatens the honor and power of Russia, which could well have waited for the result of my mediation. The friendship which I have inherited from my grandfather on his death-bed for thee and thy kingdom has always been holy to me. I have remained true to Russia whenever she has been in sore straits, and especially during her last war. The peace of Europe can still be maintained by thee if Russia decides to cease her military measures, which threaten Germany and Austria-Hungary."

On July 31st the German Chancellor telegraphed to the German Ambassador at St. Petersburg: "Mobilization, however, must follow unless Russia ceases within twelve hours all warlike measures against us and Austria-Hungary, and gives us definite assurance thereof." And on August 1st the Chancellor telegraphed to his Ambassador that unless the Russian Government had given a satisfactory answer, he was at five o'clock to hand to it a declaration which culminated in the following words: "His Majesty the Emperor, my august Sovereign, in the name of the Empire, takes up the defiance and considers himself in a state of war against Russia."

The Chancellor had on July 31st wired to his Ambassador at Paris: "Mobilization inevitably means war. Kindly ask the French Government whether it will remain neutral in a Russian-German war. Answer must come within eighteen hours."

> Russia refused to answer, and the French
> Premier declared that "France would do that
> which might be required of her by her interests."
> The German Ambassador at St. Petersburg
> demanded his passports at once. But the Ger-
> man Ambassador at Paris took no overt action,
> for some tortuous reason, which was doubtless
> intimately connected with military movements.

Night of August 1st: Russian patrols attack
the German railway bridge near Eichenried and
try to surprise the German railway station at
Miloslaw. A Russian column crosses the German
frontier at Schwidden, and two squadrons of
Cossacks ride against Johannisburg.

August 1st: (at last) Germany's mobilization.

And France?

July 27th: The Fourteenth Army Corps breaks
off its maneuvers.

July 31st: General mobilization.

August 2d: French troops attack German frontier posts, cross the frontier and occupy German
towns. Bomb-throwing aviators come into Baden
and Bavaria; also, after violating Belgium's neu-
,trality by crossing Belgian territory, they enter
the Rhine Province and try to destroy bridges.

Only after all this is the German Ambassador
at Paris instructed to demand his passports.

> The ingenuousness of the writer of this German
> apologia in imagining that American readers
> would be simple enough to be worked into a state
> of indignation by his tabulation of a few minute

and utterly unproved and unlikely frontier incidents in Russia following the declaration of war,
and twaddle about French aviators violating
neutrality by flying over Belgian territory following France's rejection of the German ultimatum,
leads up to the hypocritical protest: "Only after
all this is the German Ambassador at Paris instructed to demand his passports."

The French suspected him of trying to do a
little espionage, so long was he in removing his
unwelcome presence.

And England?

In London war must already have been decided
upon by July 31st; the English Admiralty had
even before that date advised Lloyd's against
insuring German ships. On the same day the
German Government gave emphatic support in
Vienna to the English mediatory proposal of Sir
Edward Grey. But the entire English fleet had
already been assembled.

> To say that England had decided upon war by
> July 31st is one of the crudest absurdities in the
> book. The answers to the German ultimatum to
> France and Russia were not given until August
> 1st, and as there was no question of Germany's
> declaring war on Great Britain, she was not con-
> cerned until a state of war existed between her
> allies and Germany. That the Admiralty should
> warn Lloyd's not to insure German ships—the
> ships of a nation on the verge of war—was not
> very extraordinary. The statement that the Ger-
> man Government gave emphatic support in Vi-

12

enna to the English mediatory proposal on the
same day would be called an undiplomatic name
by Americans, knowing as they did long before
this wonderful book was published that Austria
got up the whole business to oblige Germany.
The entire English fleet had undoubtedly been
assembled, but America knows just as well as
Germany that it was assembled for the monster
review of their ships which the English are in
the habit of holding every July.

It may be mere coincidence that England has
been assembling her entire fleet for review every
year at the time laid down by the German War
Office as the proper moment for invading an
enemy's country, because the maximum amount
of damage can be done to its harvests. On July
31st, as I have said, British ships were already
detained in Hamburg.

Of course, English public opinion was and still
is divided. As late as August the *Daily Graphic*
wrote in reference to the Russian mobilization
order: "Will the Russian order also be carried
out in the provinces on the German frontier?
If so, then the labor of the peace-preservers is at
an end, for Germany is compelled to answer with
the mobilization of its armed forces. We confess
that we are not able to understand this attitude
of Russia, in view of the resumption of negotiations
at Vienna."

And a leaflet distributed in the streets of London
said that "a war for Russia is a war against
civilization."

As I have said, outside the Ostrich Press, the "Daily Graphic" was the only paper which questioned the wisdom of Russia in being prepared for war if she was going to exercise any restraining influence over Austria and Germany. Russia, being, according to German complaints, well served by spies, was probably aware throughout the negotiations that Germany had instigated Austria's move, and under the form of an entreaty to intervene was urging the Kaiser to reflect before he plunged Europe into war. That opinion in England is not divided has been amply proved by the National Liberal Club's inviting the Constitutional Club to join it in promoting a great recruiting meeting (in which the Labor Party took a prominent part) and by the patriotic speeches of the Irish leaders, and by thousands of Irish Nationalists singing "God Save the King" on a football ground at Belfast on Saturday, September 19th. There is nothing to prove that the leaflet mentioned in this paragraph was not paid for by Germany. Hammann's Press Bureau was equal to efforts quite as brilliant as this.

A telegram from the British Ambassador at St. Petersburg, dated August 1, 1914, establishes the fact that Germany and Austria could have been under no disillusion as to the result of Austria's persisting. "He (M. Sazanof) went on to say that during the Balkan crisis he had made it clear to the Austrian Government that war with Russia must inevitably follow an Austrian attack on Servia. It was clear that Austrian domination of Servia was as intolerable for Russia as the dependence of the Netherlands on Germany would be to Great Britain. It was, in fact, for Russia a question of life and death. The policy of Austria had throughout been both tortuous and immoral, and she thought that she could treat Russia with defiance, secure in the support of her German ally. Similarly the policy of Germany had been an equivocal and double-faced policy, and it mattered little whether the German Government knew or did not know the terms of the Austrian ultimatum; what mattered was that her intervention with the Austrian Government had been postponed until the moment had passed when its influence would have been felt."

So much as to the preparations for the war; and now we take up the conduct of the war itself.

By glancing at the foreign press during this one week we have been able to collect the following specimen pieces of news:

London: The British Admiralty reports that the British fleet had driven back the German fleet to the Dutch coast.

There is not one word of truth in this. The Admiralty itself appears later to have recovered its senses—at least, it denied a Reuter story about a "great English naval victory near the Dogger Bank." But the English manufactories of lies are already so actively at work that Members of Parliament have protested in the House itself against the "lying reports of the English press."

The British Admiralty report that the British fleet had driven back the German fleet to the

Dutch coast may not have a word of truth in it—
if it was ever issued. It is highly unlikely that
the German fleet went near enough to them to be
driven, and the Germans may have no difficulty
in proving that their fleet had never left harbor.
The British Admiralty has been most sober about
operations in the North Sea; it has preserved an
almost absolute silence about them.

Paris: From Paris the assertion was made and
disseminated throughout the world that "the
landing of English troops in Belgium; they were
enthusiastically received by the population. The
landing proceeded rapidly, and in the best order,
as the agreement between the two General Staffs
guaranteed the perfect carrying-out of the dis-
embarkment plans."

Not a single word of this is true. At present
not one English soldier has been landed.

> There was not a word in the English papers
> about the landing of English troops on the Con-
> tinent until they had been there for three days.
> The source of the information at Paris is not given,
> but it is the kind of rumor that any irresponsible
> French paper might have circulated.

In a similar way the Baltic Sea has become the
scene of invented "battles"—of "German defeats,"
of course: the Russian Baltic fleet sank a German
war vessel in a battle that never occurred.

> In the English papers it was the German Baltic
> fleet which destroyed a large Russian ship in a
> battle that never occurred off the Aland Islands.

And: "The Russian vanguard has crossed the German frontier without meeting any opposition." As a matter of fact, there is not a single Russian soldier on German soil. All inroads have been repulsed, and the German offensive has everywhere been successful.

If there was not a single Russian soldier on German soil when these lines were written, there are plenty now.

A Dutch newspaper prints the following report from France:

"*Belfort:* Many hundreds of Alsatians are joining the French army with great enthusiasm, also many Italian-Swiss. A large number of Alsace-Lorrainers are waiting near the frontier with a view of crossing it at a favorable opportunity to fight on the French side."

Such absurdity in the face of the unbroken unanimity of the entire German people and despite the manifest enthusiasm of the Alsace-Lorrainers for the German cause.

The sympathy of the Alsace-Lorrainers with France is notorious. If Bismarck had lived and remained in power, he would not have permitted the stupid tyranny and outrages which kept Alsace and Lorraine from contemplating any reconciliation with Germany. We know that just before the war Alsatians and Lorrainers attempting to go to France were murdered in cold blood. Any spies France may have in Germany, except

renegade Germans, and they cannot be many in so patriotic a country, unless they are rebels against the cruel militarism, must for linguistic reasons be Alsatians or Lorrainers. A pure Frenchman would have the greatest difficulty in passing for a German.

As to the love of Alsace and Lorraine for Germany—have they already forgotten the Zabern incident? Though Lieutenant von Förstner, the brute who began it, was the first German officer taken prisoner in the war,[1] and von Reuter, the colonel of the regiment, has been killed.

As the Italian-Swiss goes to France in large numbers in the cheap restaurant business, it is highly likely that there is an Italian-Swiss element in the French army. The Italians themselves have formed a legion to fight for France. The men of Italian descent in the Austrian army, and many thousands of them are compelled to fight and are serving against Russia, surrender whenever they get the opportunity.

Equally stupid and made up for incurably credulous readers is an official report of the French War Ministry—not a private rumor, be it noted, but an official communication. It says: "A young Frenchman reports under oath that he was arrested, along with several other Frenchmen, at the railway-station in Lörrach while on the homeward journey from Baden; and they were led through the whole city under a military escort:

[1] He has since been reported killed fighting in the German ranks, so he must have been retaken.

184 The Real Truth About Germany

One of the Frenchmen shouted 'Hurrah for France!' and was at once shot down. Three others who protested against this suffered the same fate; and so did a fifth man, who thereupon had called the Germans murderers. The rest of the Frenchmen, proceeding to Switzerland by rail, heard shots fired in the adjoining compartment; they discovered that two Italians had been shot by Germans because one had protested against the opening of the window, and another had jostled a German."

Does such stuff call for any refutation at all?

As the German soldiers in Belgium cut down women and children whenever they uttered a Belgian sentiment, the statement is probably incapable of refutation.

Any outrage short of murder might, under the circumstances, even in times of peace have happened against the Italians. But in time of war after Italy had refused to fight for Germany, the operation would have been invested with an atmosphere of holy zeal for the Fatherland.

From *The Times*, August 31st, 1914:

"The leading Italian journal, the *Corriere della Sera*, of August 21st contains the following particulars of massacres of Italians by German troops in France and Germany:

"'At Jarny (Meurthe-et-Moselle) an Italian named Bachetta kept a small café much frequented by Italian miners, Towards 8 A.M. of August 3d, several battalions of the 68th German Infantry entered Jarny, brushing aside the French defense. The Germans lost one killed and four wounded. The inhabitants of the town were immediately accused of having fired upon the German troops, whose commander ordered all the male inhabitants to assemble in the principal square. The women and children, who tried to accompany their fathers and husbands, were driven away with the butt-ends of rifles or pricked with bayonets. One Italian woman, named Trolli, who strove to prevent her husband, who was ill in bed, from being taken to the square, was severely wounded. German patrols then searched every house.

"'In the Italian café several miners' picks and other implements were found Thereupon fifteen Italians, whose names and birthplaces are given by the *Corriere della Sera*, were arrested and immediately shot. None of the Italians had offered any resistance or been guilty of any offense save the possession of their working tools.'

"The same journal publishes particulars of a massacre of Italian emigrants by German soldiers at Magdeburg. Some three thousand Italian workmen, who had been employed on railway construction at Duisburg and Cologne, were sent to Magdeburg and herded together in a barracks outside the town. On the evening of August 11th one of the workmen announced that a train would be ready next day to take them to Italy. The announcement was loudly cheered. The soldiers on guard outside the rooms ordered the Italians to be silent, but as silence could not be restored immediately, an order was given to fire. Some soldiers fired high, but others fired directly into the mass, the fusillade being continued for twenty minutes. How many Italians were killed is not known, as there were several separate rooms, to which the panic-stricken workmen were confined while the dead and wounded were removed. One of the victims was a boy of twelve years."

A typical example of how it is sought to work on public opinion by means of systematic lying is afforded by the capture of Liége.

The fact is that this Belgian stronghold, along with its forts, which contained a garrison of 20,000 men, was taken by storm on August 7th by the German troops, who fought with unparalleled bravery, and that 3000 to 4000 Belgian prisoners of war are already on their way to Germany.

Yet on August 9th—two days after the fall of Liége—a dispatch was still sent to the Dutch press, stating: "The Liége forts are still in Belgian hands."

The German cannot resist the temptation to doctor military reports and dispatches. It does not seem even to occur to him to adhere to the text of truth in them; they are merely sermons delivered against the enemy or to influence opinion at home. Persons who concocted and published Mr. John Burns's anti-war speech at the Albert Hall (a speech which J. B. never delivered) must be authorities on " systematic lying." In this matter of Liége he really had an opportunity of scoring with the plain truth. But such a proceeding seemed unnatural. The English mixed up the town of Liége with the forts from ignorance. The town itself was at the mercy of any force which determined to rush it, disregarding the zone of fire between any two of the forts, and sufficiently large to smash through the Belgian lines connecting the forts. The Germans brought up an immense force, and advancing in close formation, regardless of loss of life, soon took the town.

With this they had the opportunity of pouring derision on President, King, and Emperor, who decorated or congratulated the defense of the forts, when the town, which the forts were designed to defend, had fallen. Not content with this, they claim the reduction of the fortress a week or two before it was reduced.

And on August 8th—thirty-six hours after the fall of Liége—a dispatch was sent from Paris to the newspapers of Rome, saying: "The Germans lost 20,000 men at Liége, and asked for an armistice of twenty-four hours. Liége has not yet fallen. The English landed 100,000 men at Antwerp, who were received with jubilation by the population. President Poincaré, upon the proposal of Doumergue, the Minister of War, conferred on the city of Liége the Cross of the Legion of Honor."

Another newspaper reported as follows: "The King of England sent a congratulatory dispatch to the King of Belgium upon his victory at Liége; seven German regiments were slain."

One naturally regards any northern war news from Rome with suspicion, unless the source is mentioned. For the only news which Italy can get which does not pass through France must emanate from Germany, which allows no news favorable to the Allies to pass even to its own people. We know that the English had not landed at Antwerp, and did not cross the Channel at all till long after this date. If they had landed at Antwerp, the Germans would have had to fight every inch of their way to Brussels. But we cannot feel as certain that the Germans did not lose twenty thousand men in casualties in the assault on the strong Liége forts, which they were unable to breach till the arrival of their eleven-inch

howitzers. Trying to storm forts of this class with masses of men in close formation is a very expensive proceeding. But the slaying of seven German regiments, which contain three thousand men each, does not tally with a total loss in killed, wounded, and prisoners of twenty thousand men.

Against the congratulations to Liége upon its resistance one must set the reports of German naval victories with which the German official wireless has flooded Italy to make her join her late Allies.

At Paris itself a note of the French War Ministry —published on the evening of August 7th, Liége having fallen in the early morning of that day— mentions the resistance of Liége, and says that the forts are still holding out; that the Germans who had entered the city on Thursday by passing between the forts had evacuated it on Friday; and that the Belgian division that went to the assistance of the city had therefore not even made an attack. The official note concludes from all this that the resistance of the Belgians was seriously disturbing the plan of the Germans, who were building hopes upon a rapid success.

And four full days after the capture of Liége the French Minister at Berne reported officially: "Liége has not yet been taken; the German troops were repulsed."

There does not seem to be any difference of merit or demerit between the French, who spoke of the fortress as if it was the town, and the Ger-

mans, who spoke of the town as if it was the
fortress, except that the Germans knew that they
were throwing dust in the eyes of the public, and
the French possibly did not. Of one thing there is
not the smallest doubt, and that is that the resistance of the Belgians did seriously disturb the
plan of the Germans by delaying their operations
against France for a fortnight.

At Copenhagen the following dispatches were
published: "The English and French troops had
effected a junction with the Belgian army, and
had entered Liége and made many German prisoners, among them a nephew of the German
Kaiser."

Copenhagen is one of the chief magazines of
German lies. It is humorous that a French or
Belgian lie should have varied the monotony. In
view of recent revelations one has a shrewd idea
that these reports emanated from a German
source which hid itself under the name of "Paris."

Similarly at Stockholm: "The Germans had
suffered a severe repulse."

This reads like a German wireless telegram in
which the word Germans has been substituted
by mistake for French or Russians.

Again a dispatch from Paris to Rome: "The
Germans had been driven back behind the Moselle
and were begging for an armistice; the French had
passed Namur and were pressing forward in forced
marches, while 500,000 English were falling upon
the German flank."

Rome, in this instance, must have felt the need of something sensational to balance the German fiction with which she was supplied, and invented some news and labelled it "Paris." Every newspaper of the least importance in Europe has been aware for many years that the English expeditionary army only consisted of about a hundred and fifty thousand men. If they had had five hundred thousand there would have been no war. Even the Prussian military chiefs, arrogant as they were, would not have wished to attack France and Russia with half a million English on their flank, or have contemplated entering Belgium when it would have meant the landing of this enormous English army.

Still another official report from Paris: "Liége is becoming the grave of the 150,000 Germans who are breaking their heads against its walls; the Belgians had taken 3000 prisoners, who were in a terrible condition; but for their good fortune of falling into captivity they would have starved to death."

In contrast to all this let us take the unvarnished truth as in the reported simple words of the German Quartermaster-General: "We are now able to report upon Liége without doing any harm. . . . We had only a weak force at Liége four days ago, for it is not possible to prepare for such a bold undertaking by collecting large masses of men. That we attained the desired end in spite of this is due to the excellent preparation, the valor of our troops, their energetic leadership, and the help of God. The courage of the enemy was broken, and his troops fought badly. The difficulties against us lay in the exceedingly unfavorable topography of the surroundings, which consisted of hills and woods, and in the treacherous participation of the entire population in the fighting, not even excluding women. The people fired upon our troops from ambush, from villages and forests—fired upon our physicians who were treating the wounded, and upon the wounded themselves. Hard and bitter fighting occurred; whole villages had to be destroyed in order to break the resistance, before our brave troops penetrated the girdle of forts and took possession of the city. It is true that a part of the forts still held out, but they no longer fired. The Kaiser did not want to waste a drop of blood in storming the forts, which no longer hindered the carrying out of our plans. We were able to await the arrival of heavy artillery to level the forts one after the other at our leisure, and without the sacrifice of a single life—in case their garrisons should not surrender sooner. . . . So far as can be judged at present the Belgians had more men for the defense of the city than we had for storming it. Every expert can measure from this fact the greatness of our achievement; it is without a parallel. . . .

" (Signed) von Stein,
"Quartermaster-General."

The Quartermaster-General von Stein has a name which has since become very familiar, owing to his accidentally telling the truth about the German defeat on the Marne. He announced that several thousand Germans and fifty of their guns had been captured. The effect on Germany was so bad that he was severely censured. He hastened to say that the Germans had not lost fifty guns and those thousands of prisoners, but that he meant that they had taken that number from the French. He was not truthful; the Germans had lost fifty guns.

Here also von Stein lets the truth out of the bag. He admits that it was not true that all the forts had surrendered—that some of them still held out, but no longer fired, which meant that they were reserving their ammunition until the Germans sent up their heavy masses to try again to storm them. No sane man will quarrel with the Kaiser for ordering them to be left alone until the heavy guns came up which could reduce them without loss of life. There is a characteristic von Stein note at the end of the report, in which he believes that the Belgians had larger forces at Liége than the Germans.

It is not the German people alone that will have cause to remember Liége; the whole world will do well to learn from the case of Liége that an organized manufactory of lies is trying to deceive the public opinion of all the nations. Glorious victories are converted into "defeats with heavy losses," and the strong moral discipline of the

German troops is slanderously described in the reports of the imaginative, phrase-loving French as cruelty—just as, in 1870, the Prussian Uhlans were described as thrusting through with their lances all the French babies and pinning them fast to the walls.

> The enemies of Germany will certainly have reason to remember Liége, not only as a piace whose valiant resistance had a great effect in upsetting the German plans for taking France by surprise, but as a place where they got, to use the schoolboy's phrase, "an awful sell." They certainly thought that Liége could laugh at the German attack until the English and French had time to come up and relieve it. In the face of the outrages they committed at Louvain, Dinant, and Termonde, the fact that the Uhlans did not play tent-pegging with the Belgian babies while their officers attended to burning the town, is to be ascribed not so much to the strong moral discipline of the German troops as to the fact that if they could make Belgium a German province, Liége, with its manufactories for weapons and locomotive engines, would become one of the chief manufacturing towns of the German Empire. To burn Liége would not be burning an adored national monument of the enemy, but burning bank-notes which could be converted into gold at sight.

How far the *grande nation* has already degenerated, and how far the Belgian population, akin to the French both in blood and in sentiments,

13

imitate the French in their Balkan brutality, is illustrated by two examples. One of these, in the form of a German official warning, says: "The reports at hand about the fighting around Liége show that the population of the country took part in the battle. Our troops were fired upon from ambush. Physicians were shot at while following their profession. Cruelties were practised by the population on wounded soldiers. There is also news at hand showing that German patrols in the vicinity of Metz were fired at from ambush from the French side."

"Franc tireur" accusations were part of the German plan of campaign in 1870, and were so useful that they form a much more prominent part this time. The population are terrorized by wholesale executions and burnings, on the paltriest evidence, for sniping. The English, on the other hand, allowed the largest latitude to the enemy in this respect in the Boer War. Innumerable German outrages against the Red Cross are reported.

"It may be that these occurrences are due to the composition of the population in those industrial regions, but it may also be that France and Belgium are preparing for a guerrilla warfare upon our troops. If the latter alternative should prove true, and this proof be strengthened through repetitions of these occurrences, then our opponents will have themselves to thank if this war be carried on with unrelenting severity even against the guilty population. The German troops, who are accustomed to preserve discipline and to wage war only against the armed forces of the hostile state, cannot be blamed if, in just self-defense, they give no quarter. The hope of influencing the result of the war by turning loose the passions of the populace will be frustrated by the unshaken energy of our leaders and our troops. Before neutral foreign countries, however, it must be demonstrated, even at the beginning of this war, that it was not the German troops who caused the war to take on such forms."

The details of the cruelties, here only hinted at on the Belgian and French side, are supplied and proved by an eye-witness, a German physician, who reports: "We have experienced from the Belgian population, from men, women, and half-grown boys, such things as we had hitherto seen only in wars with negroes. The Belgian civilian population shoots in blind hatred from every house, from every thick bush, at everything that is German. We had on the very first day many dead and wounded, caused by the civilian population."

The writer of the pamphlet assumes that the stories about civilians attacking troops are true, and says that it may be " due to the composition of the population in those industrial regions," or may be due to France and Belgium having determined on a system of guerrilla warfare, in which case war is to be " carried on with un-

relenting severity even against the guilty population." Doubtless Louvain represents the
German militarists' idea of severity, but even
German troops can forget themselves sometimes.
" Accustomed as they were to preserve discipline
and wage war only against the armed forces of
the hostile state," when they were driven back
from Paris they wrecked the furniture of all the
châteaux of the Marne, and broke into the wine-
stores of all the great growers of champagne.

The report that in the mining districts of Belgium, by way of discouraging the resistance of
civilians, they filled up the mine-shafts when the
miners were down in the mines has had a greater
influence in promoting the recruiting among the
miners of Northumberland and Yorkshire than
any feeling of patriotism for their country. Officers, before they countenance measures of vengeance against civilians taking part in warfare,
should remember that where large national
questions may leave a socialistic population like
miners quite cold, a fiendish piece of cruelty to
one of their own class in the exercise of his
profession may light a flame which is never
extinguished.

"Women take part as well as men. One German had his throat cut at night while in bed.
Five wounded Germans were put into a house
bearing the flag of the Red Cross; by the next
morning they had all been stabbed to death. In
a village near Verviers we found the body of one
of our soldiers with his hands bound behind his

back and his eyes punched out. An automobile
column which set out from Liége halted in a
village; a young woman came up, suddenly drew
a revolver, and shot a chauffeur dead. At Em-
merich, an hour by foot from Aachen, a sanitary
automobile column was attacked by the populace
on a large scale and fired at from the houses.
The Red Cross on our sleeves and on our auto-
mobiles gives us physicians no protection at all."

The Germans seem to have forgotten that the
Flemings are of the same blood as the Boers, and
that the Belgian papers reprinted the rapturous
applause with which any outrage committed by
the Boers against British stragglers, or under a
treacherous use of the white flag, or in any other
way, was received by the German Press. That
was blessed by the eternal spirit of freedom, that
was inspiring a small Power to a heroic resistance
against a big bully. It was unfortunate that the
Belgians should see the matter in exactly the
same light as the Boers. I think that the English
may in fairness admit that the Belgian peasantry,
when the war began, did not understand, and
very likely could not be made to understand, that
they must not fight tooth and nail against the
invader. But the Germans should have been
satisfied with the same punishment as the English meted out in cases of genuine treachery in
the South African war—to burn the house or farm
from which the shot came, not the whole town,
and to shoot anyone caught committing a murder
or destroying a railway line or anything else

which might cause death to the English troops.
The English allowed men without uniform to
band together for the defense of their village.
They only punished treachery, and this is one
of the principal causes which has made the
Dutch in South Africa so loyal to the English in
the present crisis. They have no ineffaceable
memories.

Enemies on all sides! With dishonorable weapons against us, and with documentary lies for the
rest of the world! Let us calmly allow them to
continue lying and slandering as they have begun
—it will result finally in injuring themselves.
The world will very soon see through this impudent, unabashed game; and it will finally side with
the people which keeps to the truth. Only the
weakling lies and swindles; the strong man loves
and honors truth. Let us act like the strong man
in the struggle!

It is very unkind of the writers of this book to
apply such hard names to the German Ambassador in the United States. Surely he will resent
their describing his efforts on their behalf as
" this impudent unabashed game," and being
called a " weakling "? Is it not a military offense
to use such language of von Stein, Quartermaster-
General of the German Army? These two men
have done their best and, as far as one can make
out, are acting under instructions from higher
quarters.

To be serious, the writers of this book can have
no sense of humor when they talk of documen-

tary lies for the rest of the world—while the rest
of the world is pouring derision on the wireless
messages sent out by the German official lies
bureau, and even Holland, on which they can
exercise most pressure, refuses to print them any
longer. Nothing is more certain than that American opinion will finally side with the people which
keeps to the truth. It knows to-day that the official report from Russia which says that Austria has
lost two hundred and fifty thousand men in killed
and wounded and a hundred thousand in prisoners is true; and it cannot have the same respect
for the Wolff Agency. A Swiss paper has taken
the trouble to add up the losses of the Allies in
the Wolff reports, and finds that " the French
have up to the present lost 880,000 men in killed
and prisoners.

" The Germans claim to have captured: 177
generals, 1213 flags, and 11,982 cannons.

" According to the agency, the British army has
already been annihilated twice, and as for the
Russians, the Germans · claim to have made
800,000 of them prisoners, and conducted them to
Berlin."

The Wolff Agency is the go-between which has
endeavored to bring the Havas Agency, Reuter's
and the other telegraphic services of the world
into line with the Hammann Official Press Bureau
in Berlin. The two agencies named hastened to
repudiate the statement so far as they are concerned. Some day even the Canary Press[1] will
turn.

[1] Hammann takes care to keep a paper in the Canary Islands
au courant, with wireless.

FOREWORD TO CHAPTER IX

The Times, August 8th, 1914:

"FRENCH AMBASSADOR INSULTED."

"JOURNEY TO FRONTIER."

". . . After being refused permission to leave Germany through Holland or Belgium, as he intended, he accepted an offer to travel through Vienna, but a few hours later received from an official of the German Foreign Office a notification that he and the staff of the Embassy would be taken to Denmark, though it might be impossible for him to obtain a passage from Denmark to England or France. . . . The journey to Denmark lasted more than twenty-four hours. No food was provided. On nearing the Kiel Canal soldiers entered the train; windows were ordered to be pulled up, and blinds were drawn. The Ambassador and his staff, as well as the ladies and children, were ordered to remain motionless and not to attempt to touch their hand baggage. A soldier was placed at the door of each compartment with a revolver in his hand and his finger on the trigger. After having been treated almost as a prisoner in Berlin, the Ambassador was treated in the train as a dangerous individual.

"Shortly before reaching the frontier the Ambassador was informed that the train would not proceed unless he paid immediately for the cost of it. He was told that the amount would be approximately 5000 f. (£200). In payment he drew a cheque for that amount on one of the principal Berlin banks. It was refused, and immediate payment in gold was demanded. With great difficulty the sum was collected in gold from the various members of the staff and from the Russian Consul-General at Darmstadt. On receiving the cash the German officer in command of the train, Major von Rheinbahen, gave his word of honor that the journey would be completed."

CHAPTER IX

GERMANY AND THE FOREIGNER

RESPECT FOR THE FOREIGNER—RUSSIANS WILLING
TO REMAIN IN GERMANY—ILL-TREATMENT OF
GERMANS IN BELGIUM AND FRANCE

RESPECT for the foreigner, protection for his person and property have at all times been considered sacred among civilized people. Germany can without exaggeration claim to have upheld this respect and this protection in these fateful days. Except for a few insignificant incidents which took place in several large cities, where the natural excitement of the people and the legitimate defense against an insolent system of spying led to the molesting and arrest of foreigners—mostly Russians—the measures taken against the citizens of hostile nations did not exceed what was absolutely necessary to the safety of the country.

Among the insignificant incidents which took place in large cities may be mentioned the treatment of a British Consul, who comes of a family famous in our diplomatic service, at one of the chief seaports of Germany. He and his wife and

201

his daughter were invited by one of the chief officials to a friendly dinner. While they were at dinner a man came in with a letter. The official smiled and tossed off a glass of champagne; then he smiled again and tossed off another glass of champagne; then he smiled again and tossed off a third glass. By that time he was thoroughly excited, and cried out: "Yes, the best of news! War is declared." Then he turned to the Consul and his wife and daughter, and called them dogs and pigs and reptiles, and rang the bell and sent for soldiers, who dragged them away and spat all over the Consul's wife. They took them to a prison where they threw them into a filthy room with thieves and criminals. They left them there for two days without any food or water or sanitary arrangements. Then they dragged them out again and pushed them into a train, still without any food or drink. The train went on and on, until they were bundled out at a station to change trains. The daughter was by this time so exhausted that she was nearly dying. Looking for someone to save her life, she saw a Red Cross nurse attending to someone, and implored her to give her a drink of water. The German nurse turned round and called them "Dogs of English," and said that she would rather die than do it.

The Imperial Government and likewise the Federate States have refrained from expelling *en masse* Frenchmen, Russians, Belgians, and Englishmen. It was, of course, unavoidable to take measures for the detention of such persons as

seemed suspicious and for the internation of
strangers liable to be called to take arms against
Germany.   This took place in cities, *e. g.*, Berlin,
where these men were taken away as "prisoners
of war," as soon as the "state of war" had been
proclaimed, and placed in special rooms or camps.
Lodgings and food such as seem requisite were
provided and the treatment of these prisoners is,
according to their own opinion, very kind.

> **The Germans pride themselves on having
> refrained from expelling " en masse " the male
> subjects of the Allies.   They have more than re-
> frained.   Quite elderly men—persons of Euro-
> pean reputation—were unable to get away, as well
> as enemies of military age, whom all states de-
> tain in war.   Their treatment seems to have been
> quite fair.**

The Russian agricultural laborers constitute a
special group of foreigners in Germany: there are
about 40,000–50,000 of them, men and women.

From various parts of the country, it is unanimously announced that these people are very
glad not to be obliged to return to Russia.   They
are glad to remain in Germany, and willingly
continue their work of gathering the rich German
grain, potato, and hay crops.   Should there be
any difficulties, these workmen would also have
to be interned.

> **There were, according to this account, when
> war broke out, forty or fifty thousand of these
> Russians who had not obeyed the caution sent**

> them from their country to get out of Germany. Whether they are willing or not, they have to remain there to do the harvesting as usual. There are no complaints to be made about the general treatment of the women and children of the enemy who happen to be in Germany. In some places they receive a great deal of rudeness, in others infinite kindness, but they are never, I believe, maltreated.

No measures at all have been taken against women and children belonging to hostile states. They are left free to move about as they wish. Should they remain in Germany they can be sure that they will be subject to no other inconvenience except such as the general state of war inflicts upon Germans. The authorities will protect their persons, and their private property is respected. Nobody will touch it—as nobody has touched it so far.

> The reports of the treatment of neutrals vary. Americans were at first frequently taken for English people, and suffered accordingly. Many Americans who have come over to England are boiling with indignation at the treatment which they have received, and these people, returning to America, are thorns in the side of " Count John Bernstorff " and the German-Jews who run the German-American papers and are organizing a Press campaign to influence American opinion in favor of Germany. The other Jewish papers are among the most severe critics of German militarism.

If the German people and the German Government consider the respect they owe the foreigner as a sacred law, even though the foreigner belongs to the enemy, this respect is enhanced by affection and gratitude in the case of foreigners whose countries are friendly or neutral. Thousands and thousands of Americans, Swiss, Dutch, Italians, and Scandinavians are still living in German countries. They may be sure that they live as freely here as any German citizen. Should it be possible for them to return home, the best wishes will accompany them. The property they leave here will be protected. This is guaranteed by the authorities and by influential private persons. Should they stay in Germany, however, the German people will express their sense of gratitude for any friendly help they may lend, by increased respect and protection.

According to the American refugees, the German treatment of all foreigners except neutrals of nations whom they were trying to conciliate was very bad indeed. The full brutality of Prussian militarism was turned upon these unfortunate people. A short time after the war broke out, the Kaiser, desperately conscious of the isolation of Germany, gave orders that the Americans and the Dutch and the Swiss were to be conciliated in every possible way. The Swiss are allowed to import the food supplies and coal supplies which they draw from Germany as usual, and the Dutch are allowed to pass in and out of Germany, in

uniform or plain clothes, as they please, and are
allowed to use bicycles, motor-cycles, and motors
with a freedom from restriction and red-tape
which they have never enjoyed in their lives
before in Germany. The Swiss are specially
favored, because there seems to be no doubt that
the Kaiser meant to throw a force through Switzerland on France, and was confronted by such a
force that he was frightened and drew back.
The Swiss were suspicious of his intentions, and
had two hundred thousand men ready, which, in
an impregnable country like Switzerland, was far
too big a bite even for the Kaiser. He has been
especially anxious to efface the memory of the
Basle incident. The Swiss are glad to enjoy
favors, but remain ready to strike on any real
provocation.

As to the Italians, they have been treated quite
as badly as the English or French—are being
punished, in fact, for not declaring war on Germany's side. Immense pressure has been
brought upon them to change their minds, and
should they do so, there will doubtless be a
marked difference in the treatment of the Italians
in Germany. The bid for Italian support is shown
by the swarm of German commercial travelers
in Italy who are offering Italian shopkeepers
impossible discounts, impossible terms of credit,
and delivery with unheard-of dispatch.

A strong contrast is noticeable between Germany's attitude towards foreigners and the facts
revealed just now as to the treatment meted out

in inimical countries not only to Germans but to other foreigners. Truly, in *England*, there has been some effort to act according to the usages of civilized nations when engaged in warfare. Germans and Austrians, have been insulted and molested; there has been some occasional destruction of property in stores; but, as far as can be judged, these were excesses of an uncontrollable mob. A general expulsion has not been ordered, and it is to be hoped that the Germans living in the United Kingdom and in its colonies will not suffer too heavy damages, in person or in property.

Germany allows England one merit: whereas other countries except Germany are behaving very badly to enemies " and other foreigners," England has made some effort to act as a civilized nation. Germans and Austrians have been insulted and molested, and their stores occasionally wrecked. This, it may be remarked, was not due to wantonness on the part of the mob, but was solely where the proprietor could not deny himself the pleasure of insulting the English, or was trying to make a " famine " profit out of the war.
It acknowledges that Germans and Austrians have not been expelled. Since they have not they ought to be in concentration camps. It is certainly wrong that there should be any of the fighting age, or otherwise able to do damage, at large in England, and the fact that many hotel-managers and waiters—a larger percentage of the former has not suffered—are still employed, and an immense number of Germans are still

controlling various businesses in London and elsewhere, is wrong and dangerous. An exact account of their property should be taken, so that it may be restored to them intact after the war, and where they have businesses, these should be placed in the hands of official receivers or trustees.

Russia, France, and Belgium on the other hand, have by the ill-treatment and plundering of foreigners living in their countries, struck themselves out of the list of civilized nations. Innumerable reports from expelled or fugitive people prove this, and official reports confirm them. Also the press of neutral, neighboring countries, such as Switzerland, Holland, and Italy is full of similar complaints. Owing to the scarcity of news from Russia, the facts known so far only concern St. Petersburg, where German and Austrian men and women, residents or transients, were beaten or stoned in the streets. Here were also some cruel mutilations and murders

It is certain that Russia, France, and Belgium have not ill-treated any foreigners except their enemies, and there is strong evidence to prove that the numerous Germans in Antwerp were being well treated until it was discovered that practically all of them were serving the enemy in some treacherous way or other, like the German at Zanzibar who sent a message to the "Koenigsberg" that the "Pegasus" was undergoing repairs and unable to get up steam. Then the Belgian indignation became very strong, but none of the alleged barbarities appear to have been true.

Austrians and Germans were not turned out of Paris until the siege of Paris appeared to be imminent at the beginning of September. So many were expelled then that there could have been no general expulsion before.

Russia keeps her affairs to herself, but the behavior of her soldiers in the field has been so good compared with that of the Germans that there is no reason why she should have behaved badly to German and Austrian residents. Indeed, her police arrangements are so thorough, that it may have been possible to allow them their usual liberties.

To say that Switzerland, Holland, and Italy are full of complaints about the behavior of the Allies is one of the most colossal falsehoods in a book where they grow large. The Italians have not moved out of France or England, the only two countries in which there are any great number of them. They have been living entirely unmolested and on such cordial terms that they have been holding huge meetings to enlist Italian legions to serve in the English and French armies.

The relations between Switzerland and France and Italy and France are so cordial that the French have withdrawn nearly all their garrisoning forces on the Swiss and Italian borders.

Holland is chiefly concerned with Belgium, and Germany knows better than anyone else how cordial the relations of the two countries are, and how furious the Dutch are over the German atrocities in Belgium.

The beautiful building of the German Embassy in St. Petersburg was attacked by the mob. And the police watched all these misdeeds with crossed arms or even assisted. Probably what took place in Petersburg also occurred in other Russian cities; we shall soon know.

The appended cutting from "The Times" shows how justified the Russians were in raiding the German Embassy at St. Petersburg. Using the Embassy for the distribution of weapons and seditious literature is one of the most disgraceful episodes in the history of diplomacy.

The Times, August 8th, 1914:
"St. Petersburg, August 7th.
"The outrage on the German Embassy has brought a strange aftermath. From trustworthy witnesses I hear that large quantities of rifles, revolvers, and seditious proclamations were discovered by the wreckers. It looks as if the German Embassy had been used as a secret center for revolutionary propaganda."

There are a great many complaints against the French and the Belgians. On the evening of August 1st, the mobilization was announced, and the next morning the official order was posted on the walls that within twenty-four hours from the beginning of the day, all Germans and Austrians, irrespective of age, sex, or profession, would have to leave France. Those who remained and could not reach the boundary would be taken to the southwestern part of the country and imprisoned.

As mentioned on the preceding page, there is the plainest evidence that German and Austrians

**were not expelled from France on the 1st August,
because a general expulsion of them from Paris
had to be proclaimed a month later, when Paris
feared a siege.**

There were few trains tor Belgium or Switzerland. Thousands and thousands who had to
abandon their property, rushed to the stations
with wife and children, fought for room in the
overcrowded trains, surrounded by a howling
mob, and even then were punched and slapped by
policemen. During the trip there was nothing
but misery. Men and women fell ill, children
died. The refugees had to cross the Belgian
boundary, walking a distance of 6–7 kilometers
in the middle of the night, dead-tired, their lug-
gage stolen—sometimes, it is said, by officials.
In Belgium the same tragedy occurred as in France.

**With his usual total lack of humor and im-
agination, the writer of this egregious book describes what happened in Germany to the French
and other enemies, and says that this is the
way in which the French behaved to the Germans.**

And then came the salvation. The cordial,
hospitable reception by the Germans in Holland
and Switzerland is unanimously praised and
appreciated.

**Holland is rather suspected of having shown
special favor to Germans, but it is difficult not
to be kind and courteous to a burglar who holds
a loaded automatic pistol to your head. The**

Dutch doubtless had to deserve all the nice things which the Germans say about their behavior.

The Swiss seem to have behaved well to all foreigners, but as Switzerland was at peace with all of them, and Switzerland's national business of keeping hotels and pensions depends on having a plentiful supply of the raw material in the shape of foreigners requiring accommodation, there is no reason why Switzerland should not have welcomed them. But Switzerland was not only glad to receive all the foreigners who had been turned out of any country and could pay for their accommodation. The Swiss felt that humanity compelled them to charge exiles the lowest possible prices, though the refugees would not get bedrooms in the finest and most expensive hotels for a shilling a night, like they can in Berlin. One admires the Germans very much if this is true, as is alleged; there must be many refugees in Berlin, and to give them rooms at this moderate price strikes me as being magnificent.

The reports of brutal acts from Paris, Antwerp, Brussels would be incredible, were they not confirmed hundred-fold. The most brutal and insulting threats of death were flung by processions of people going through the streets, to all those who looked like foreigners. They were severely ill-treated. Houses and stores were upset, furniture and the like was thrown into the streets, employees and working people were dragged out, women were stripped and pushed through the

streets, children were thrown out of windows.
Knives, swords, sticks, and revolvers were used.
One could fill books with the details, but they are
all equally cruel.   Not only Germans and Austrians were expelled and ill-treated, but citizens of
neutral states shared this awful lot.   Thousands
of Italians were expelled, as well as numerous
Rumanians.   The press in both countries complains bitterly and asks what has become of those
who remained in France and were imprisoned in
the South—but nobody knows.

**The details of brutalities in Paris, Antwerp, and
Brussels are, in most of their viler and more
picturesque aspects, fictions of the fertile brain
of Hammann and the papers and people whom he
hires to " invent " for the German authorities—
the people who have made " wireless " almost
synonymous with " false " in the matter of news.
If the writer of this book, in repeating the fictions
of Hammannias, had confined himself to Germans
and Austrians, he might have had some chance
of being believed, because Hammannias would
have supplied him—with Germans, at any rate,
who would have given their evidence according
to the directions of the Bureau; if he could not
have got Germans from Paris and Antwerp and
Brussels, he would have got Germans from his
office, and the world would not have known that
they had never left Berlin.   There were really
great openings in this direction, but in an un-
guarded moment he added: " Citizens of neutral
States shared this awful lot.   Thousands of**

Italians were expelled as well as numerous Rumanians."

The writer of this book is one of the most foolish liars I ever had to criticize. We know—and he knows, if he knows anything of current events—that the Governments of Italy and Rumania can hardly prevent their people from taking up arms for France and Belgium and " their great Allies, England and Russia." If thousands of Italians and Rumanians have been subjected to such awful treatment by the French and Belgians, why are the Italians and Rumanians straining at the leash to fight for these countries against the good neighbors of Germany and Austria? Why is the press in Italy trying to lash the Government into declaring war against Austria and Germany for the peoples who have oppressed them so cruelly?

If what he says about Italians and Rumanians is so palpably and absolutely untrue, why does the writer deserve any credence in what he has to say about their fellow-victims from Germany and Austria? Ananias might have written it himself.

History will place this ill-treatment and oppression of foreigners on record. The responsibility rests not with an uncontrollable mob, but with the Government and the authorities of the two countries who have always boasted of their culture.

If Germans and Austrians were so badly treated in France and Belgium, and the responsibility rests not with the mobs but with the Governments and authorities, cannot the destruction and massacres at Louvain, Dinant, and Termonde, and the bombarding of the incomparable Cathedral of Rheims, be traced directly to the Kaiser's order to employ " frightfulness " (of outrages, behavior, etc.) for terrorizing the peoples of invaded countries? The German military commanders who actually gave the word for these destructions would never have done so if they had expected the disapproval of the Kaiser. He is said to have given special orders to his Zeppelins to try and drop bombs upon Oxford, so as to give England something to remember. It would have been better that the world should have gone without the picture which he has painted and the opera which he has composed—priceless as they are—than that he should do this!

FOREWORD TO CHAPTER X

There is no such thing as commerce between Germany and the United States. It has ceased to exist. The Americans will themselves manufacture the raw materials, which they have hitherto been selling to Germany, and will supply the customers, who have hitherto been buying from Germany.

CHAPTER X

GERMANY'S FINANCIAL RISE SINCE 1870—EXPORT
AND IMPORT WITH THE U. S. A.—THE PRESENT
FIRM CONDITION OF GERMAN FINANCE

POLITICIANS and commercial men must base their plans upon facts, as they are, and not as they wish they were, otherwise they fail. France has closed its eyes not only to the great intellectual and moral assets of Germany, but also to its commercial resources.

> **The foolish person (or persons) who wrote this book appears to be ignorant that Germany's commercial development is largely due to money borrowed from France. One could understand France being blind to the "moral assets" of Germany, but she must know something of the commerce carried on with her money.**

France has repeatedly declared that Germany could not effect a serious political opposition, because a war would result in the ruin of its commercial and financial strength. This we heard in the Morocco crises, also in the Balkan wars.

It was owing to Germany's having to compromise the last Morocco crisis because England, and especially France and Russia, called in their money, that Germany took care to secure her own finances, and try and wreck other people's, before she put into execution the carefully-laid plot to force on a European war this summer by making Austria demand from Servia what could not be given without Russia's declaring war.

From the British Ambassador in Vienna's report, it is quite clear that Germany forced on the war as suddenly as kicking over a bucket, when Austria realized that if she did not withdraw she would have Russia on her, without a doubt. Nor, considering that Austria has lost three hundred and fifty thousand men in fighting Russia and another fifty thousand in fighting Servia, can she be blamed for having qualms. On August 1st, the very day that Germany declared war on Russia, the Austrian Ambassador informed Sir Edward Grey that Austria had neither "banged the door" on compromise nor cut off the conversations. Austria did not declare war on Russia till August 6th, and the French Ambassador at Vienna did not demand his passports till August 12th, and Great Britain informed the Austrian Ambassador that a state of war would exist between the two countries from midnight of the same day. But the report of the British Ambassador at Vienna shows that Austria kept all the Ambassadors, except Germany's, completely in the dark till her ultimatum against Servia was launched. She doubtless believed

**that the Powers of the Triple Entente were too
unready for war to object to the "fait accompli."**

Germany's love of peace, which was tested in
the above-mentioned cases, strengthened the
French in their error. He, however, who has
taken the trouble to visit Germany and the Germans in their places of employment—and especially Americans in recent years have done this,
however also many English,[1] who in vain have
protested against the war with Germany—he can
testify to the astonishing commercial advancement which Germany has made since its political
union by Bismarck.

**The error of the French lay in their imagining
that Germany had a love of peace. The writer
of this book only shows an astonishing ignorance
of the world when he supposes that any
Government was blind to "the astonishing commercial advancement of Germany."**

A few facts and statistics may recall this to
memory. The population of Germany has, since
1870, immigrants excluded, increased from forty
millions to sixty-seven millions, round numbers.
Incomes and wages in particular have approximately doubled during the last generation; sav-
ings-deposits have increased sixfold. Although,
only a generation ago, commerce and trade employed only about two fifths of the population,
now more than three fifths are engaged in this

[1] This is German English-grammar.

field of work, and Germany, as a result of its agricultural economy and increased intense farming, is to-day the third largest agricultural country of the world. In the coal and iron industries, Germany is second only to America. In one generation its coal production increased two and a half fold, its iron production almost fourfold. During the same period of time the capital of the German banks increased fourfold and their reserve-fund eightfold. Characteristic of Germany is the fact that hand in hand with this active private initiative is a strong feeling for the great universal interests and for organic coöperation of private and state resources. This feeling explains the perfect working of our state activities, in particular our railways, 95 per cent. of which are owned by the Government, and which yield essentially higher revenues than those in England or France; it explains further the willing assumption of the great financial burdens which general insurance imposes upon those engaged in private enterprises, and which to-day is proving a blessing to almost the entire laboring force of Germany, to an extent which has not yet been realized by any other country.

We may take it for granted that the writer is for once talking both sense and truth when he puts down the population of Germany at sixty-seven millions in round numbers. We need not dispute the vulgar fractions he employs in saying what proportion of Germans are engaged in

agriculture, and what in manufacture and trade.
We will allow him to say what he likes about the
increases in German banks, without dispute, unless we are thinking of investing in them.

We have nothing but admiration for the organic
coöperation of private and state resources and
private and state activities in German commerce
and manufactures. We believe that England
could not do better in this and many other phases
of commerce than imitate the noble and patriotic
example of Germany.

That the German Government has created in
less than half a century such a mighty commercial
fabric will redound to its credit forever.

What economic value to the world has a nation
which for more than forty years has concentrated
all its energy in peaceful industry? Does anyone
deny that Germany's great technical and commercial advancement has been a blessing in respect
to the development of the world? Has not the
commercial advancement in Germany had the
effect of awaking new productive powers in all
parts of the world and of adding new territories
which engage in the exchange of goods with the
civilized nations of the world?

But it is not so clear that the great technical
and commercial advancement of Germany has
been a blessing in the development of the world.
As far as England and the United States are
concerned, she may have started all sorts of
new lines in commerce and taught more nations

of savages to buy European goods; but it has all been done to benefit Germany, and, as far as she has had the power, in her own territories and colonies, she has done her best to exclude British products, and in other countries, especially in the British Islands, she has done her best to ruin English manufacturers by underselling. She has done more harm to English manufacturers than any country in the world. If German manufacturers are ruined by the war, or excluded from British possessions, the trade of Great Britain would leap up by tens of millions. And if in addition to the disappearance of German manufacturers from the market, the German shipping business is killed, Great Britain and the United States will benefit almost beyond the dreams of avarice. Has not the writer of this paragraph thought of that?

Since the founding of the new German Empire German foreign trade has increased from five and one half to approximately twenty billion marks. Germany has become the best customer of a great number of countries. Not only has the German consumption of provisions and luxuries increased in an unusual degree, also that of meat, tropical fruits, sugar, tobacco, and colonial products, but above all else that of raw materials, such as coal, iron, copper and other metals, cotton, petroleum, wool, skins, etc. Germany furnished a market for articles of manufacture also, for American machinery, English wool, French luxury articles, etc. One is absolutely wrong in the belief that the

competition of German industry in the world
market has been detrimental to other commercial
nations. Legitimate competition increased the
business of all concerned.

> I have no doubt that the figures given of the
> increase of German foreign trade since the found-
> ing of the new empire are substantially accurate;
> but, when he talks of Germany being the best
> customer of a great number of countries, he
> omits to emphasize the fact that with the ex-
> ception of French luxury articles and American
> machinery, nearly every German import which
> he mentions in this paragraph is either of raw
> materials or something which Germany cannot
> produce.   If England, for instance, ceased to sell
> Germany coal, of which she ought not to sell her
> a single ton, what would England's exports to
> Germany look like?—especially if raw wool were
> also deducted, and reserved for manufacture by
> Yorkshire mills.
>
> The competition of German industry may not
> have been detrimental to some nations, but to
> England it has been homicidal, and if the war
> should end, as we hope and believe, in the de-
> struction of the German power, the putting back
> German manufacture, commerce, and shipping
> for half a century will be worth any sum of
> money which the war costs to England.

The United States of America has reaped especial
profit from Germany's flourishing commercial conditions.   Germany purchases more from the United
States of America than from any other country of

the world. Germany buys annually from the United States of America approximately $170,000,000 worth of cotton, $75,000,000 worth of copper, $60,000,000 worth of wheat, $40,000,000 animal fat, $20,000,000 mineral oil and the same amount of vegetable oil. In 1890 the import and export trade between Germany and the United States mounted to only $100,000,000, in 1913 to about $610,000,000. Germany to-day imports from the United States goods to the value of $430,000,000, while she exports to the United States nearly $180,000,000 worth. No nation therefore can judge as well as the United States what German commerce means to the world.

What profit does the United States reap from Germany's flourishing condition? If she exported thirty-six millions' worth of manufactures to Germany, instead of Germany exporting them to her, and imported the eighty-six millions' worth of raw materials from Germany instead of exporting them to Germany, the American nation would be under an obligation to Germany. As it is the boot is on the other leg.

If England is supplying her own wants and those of her Colonies, and a vastly increased proportion of the neutral markets, instead of letting Germany do it, she can take all these raw materials from the United States, and more into the bargain.

In what condition are the finances of Germany? In this field our opponents will be obliged to change their views. In 1912 Germany's national debt was about fourteen marks per capita lower than England's. The public debt of France per capita was far more than double that of Germany. Germany, however, has large national assets which offset its liabilities. For example, the stocks of the Prussian railways alone exceed by far the aggregate amount of the Prussian debt, the income of the railways alone is essentially greater than the amount which the interest and amortization of the entire state debt demand.

> If Germany's national debt is fourteen shillings per head lower than England's, assuming that it is, and only half that of France, assuming that it is, the reason is on the surface. Germany exacted two hundred millions from France as a war indemnity, and Great Britain, instead of exacting a war indemnity from the Boers, actually gave them money to enable them to get over the effects of the war. Besides, in the last ten years Germany's debt has been increasing and ours decreasing.
>
> Great Britain's railway stocks, when they are added together, present a formidable amount, and we regard them with suspicion, instead of supporting them as the Prussians support their railway stocks.

The war, which according to the French conception was destined to bring about the financial and commercial ruin of Germany, has brought forth the astonishing result that the famous French money market was the first to fail in this crisis. As early as July 25th, before the rejection of the Austrian Ultimatum by Servia had been made known, the offer of 3 per cent. redeemable French notes to the French exchange was so great that the Chambre Syndicale des Agents de Change, in the interest of the public, prohibited the quotation of a lower rate than 78 per cent., while bids of 74 per cent. had already been submitted. Sale in blank was absolutely forbidden, and in the coulisse business was at a standstill. A few days later, the July liquidation, in the official market as well as in the coulisse, was postponed until the end of August, which action proved the necessity of a period of grace. On July 31st the French savings banks, at the command of the government, suspended daily payments and paid out sums to the amount of 50 francs, fourteen days' notice being necessary.

That the war did not bring about the financial and commercial ruin of Germany directly it was declared is due to the fact that Germany knew that it was going to be declared, and did not declare it until she had rigged the money market by making every arrangement she could to conserve her own position, and sending agents with enormous sums of money—it is rumored four millions for England and two for France— to London and Paris to create such slumps that the London Stock Exchange and the Paris Bourse should break. And broken they would have been

if the plot had not been discovered. Paris led the way in meeting the crisis by prohibiting the sale of the French " rentes, " which correspond to our Consols, below a certain price, and by only allowing sums up to fifty francs to be drawn from the savings banks, and that with a fortnight's notice.

The London money market, too, has hardly stood the war test. On July 30th, the Bank of England was obliged to raise its rate of discount from 3 to 4 per cent., several days later to 8 per cent., and again after a few days to the incredible rate of 10 per cent. In contrast to this, the President of the German Reichsbank was able on the 1st of August to declare that the directorate, because of the strength of the Reichsbank and the solid constitution of the German money market, did not consider it necessary to follow England's example. The German Reichsbank has therefore not exceeded the rate of 6 per cent. Worse yet was the fact that England on August 2d was obliged to require grace on exchange and France on August 3d grace on its accounts-current and Lombard loans.

London, some days later, put the bank rate up to 10 per cent., and closed its Stock Exchange on account of the dumping of foreign shares on the London market. The wisdom of this was shown by the fact that the situation was saved, and the rate reduced in a few days to five per cent.—which our author takes care not to mention. There were two reasons why Germany did not have to make countermoves of the same magnitude. It knew that the crash was coming, having engineered it, and it did not have to meet a rush of sales of shares from other countries, because other countries were afraid to sell their shares on the Berlin Bourse, for fear that the German purchasers would default.

Although along with England and France, also Russia, Austria, Italy, Belgium, and other nations required temporary credits, Germany to date has not deemed it necessary to ask for time in meeting its obligations. Savings banks, other banks, and financial institutions are meeting all demands without restriction. The fact that the English money market, which up to the present time has been considered the financial center of international trade, has failed, will bring many a serious thought to all commercial men interested in the world market.

In other words, as Germany could not be trusted to pay for what it bought, there was not the same rush to sell shares there; and as the whole financial situation had been carefully arranged, savings banks and other banks and financial institutions were ready. The English money market did not fail; it simply closed to prevent any more members of its Stock Exchange being hammered owing to the failure of foreign clients to pay up, and to prevent the leading shares being wrecked by professional slumpers with the resources of a hostile nation behind them. To compare the real situations of the English and German money markets, one has only to contrast the way in which the war loans are being subscribed. In England as fast as an instalment is put on the market, it is subscribed three times over. The German loan appeared to be in danger of failure, because other nations would not look at it, in fact Germany openly confessed that she would get no financial assistance from neutrals. The impassioned appeals of the Press for Germans to bring out their savings seem to be falling on deaf ears. At first its chief chance of a successful flotation seemed to lie in German-American bankers putting their patriotism to the land of their extraction before their pockets.

German commerce has doubtless been temporarily injured by the war, but the *esprit de corps* and organization which animate the German nation are not only a firm foundation for German commerce, but also a strong support for the further development of the commerce and trade of the entire civilized world, if, as we hope, peace soon is reëstablished.

It would not be too much to say that German overseas commerce, with the exception of some peddling with Scandinavia, has ceased to exist. If Germany is beaten in the war, she will have to begin again from the very beginning her shipping business and all trade outside the borders of Germany.

FOREWORD TO CHAPTER XI

By the Right Hon. Winston Churchill in his great Recruiting Speech of September 11th:

"By one of those dispensations of Providence, which appeals so strongly to the German Emperor—(laughter)—the nose of the bulldog has been slanted backwards so that he can breathe without letting go. (Laughter and cheers.) We have been successful in maintaining naval control thus far in the struggle, and there are also sound reasons for believing, that as it progresses the chances in our favor will not diminish but increase. In the next twelve months the number of great ships that will be completed for this country is more than double the number which will be completed for Germany—(cheers)—and the number of cruisers three or four times as great. (Cheers.) Therefore, I think I am on solid ground when I come here to-night and say that you may count upon the naval supremacy of this country being effectively maintained as against the German Power for as long as you wish. (Cheers.) . . .

"I was reading in the newspaper the other day that the German Emperor made a speech to some of his regiments, in which he urged them to concentrate their attention upon what he was pleased to call 'French's contemptible little Army.' (Laughter.) Well, they are concentrating their attention upon it—(laughter and cheers)—and that Army, which has been fighting with such extraordinary prowess, which has revived in a fortnight of adverse actions the ancient fame and glory of our arms upon the Continent—(cheers)—and which to-night, after a long, protracted harassed, unbroken, and undaunted rearguard action—the hardest trial to which troops can be exposed—is advancing in spite of the loss of one-fifth of its numbers, and driving its enemies before it— that Army must be reinforced and backed and supported and increased and enlarged in numbers and in power by every means and every method that every one of us can employ.

"There is no reason why, if you set yourselves to it—I have not come here to make a speech of words, but to point out to you the necessary and obvious things which you can do—there is no doubt that, if you set yourselves to it, the Army which is now fighting so valiantly on your behalf and our Allies can be raised from its present position to 250,000 of the finest professional soldiers in the world, and that in the new year something like 500,000 men, and from that again, when the early summer begins in 1915, to the full figure of twenty-five Army Corps fighting in line together. The vast population of these islands, and all the Empire, is pressing forward to serve, its wealth is placed at your disposal; the Navy opens the way for the passage of men and everything necessary for the equipment of our forces. Why should we hesitate when here is the sure and certain path to ending this war in the way we mean it to end? (Cheers.)

"There is little doubt that an Army so formed will, in quality and character, in native energy, in the comprehension which each individual has of the cause for which he is fighting, exceed in merit any army in the world. We have only to have a chance of even numbers, or anything approaching even numbers, to demonstrate the superiority of free-thinking active citizens over the docile sheep who serve the ferocious ambitions of drastic kings. (Cheers.) Our enemies are now at the point which we have reached fully extended. On every front of the enormous field of conflict the pressure upon them is such that all their resources are deployed. With every addition to the growing weight of the Russian Army —(cheers)—with every addition to the forces at the disposal of Sir John French—(cheers)—the balance must sag down increasingly against them."

CHAPTER XI

WHO IS TO BE VICTORIOUS?

AN APPEAL TO AMERICAN FRIENDS

THE American citizen who is now leaving Europe, which has been turned into an enormous military camp, may consider himself fortunate that he will soon be able to set foot in the new world where he will be enabled again to take up his business pursuits. In the meantime, old Europe is being torn asunder by a terrible war among its various peoples. It will make him happy again to greet mountain and valley, field and garden, which are not threatened, nor trampled down by armies, or covered with blood; again to see cities in which business and traffic are not brought to a standstill by calling in all men capable of military service; and he may thank fortune that his people have been given room enough in which to expand and to permit them freely to unfold their power; that they are spared the great necessity of resisting the tightening ring of enemies in the east and west, on land and water, in a struggle for national existence.

Doubtless the American who has been on the continent of Europe since the war began, espe-

cially in France or Belgium, will not know how
sufficiently to thank his Creator for having removed him from all possible enemies, east or
west, by land or sea, except the pacifically-
minded sister-nation of Anglo-Saxons.

His experience will have made him feel more
than that. It will make him realize what an
accursed thing militarism is, and it may not
unlikely have inspired him with the determination to throw his power also into the scale, if
Germany, that is militarism, cannot be crushed
without it. He will say: One thing shall not
be—never again shall a continent be trampled
into a wilderness and millions of men seek each
other's deaths, with all the inventions of modern
science, to gratify the insensate ambition of one
man. " To him the German Emperor is the
modern Nero, who has been fiddling with ballet-
music while he has been preparing to burn, not
Rome, but all Europe.

But the American will feel the effects of the
fate of the old world. Even though he knows his
own country is not directly involved, he will
certainly realize that the great net of international
traffic and the progress of his country are connected by many strong ties to the life and prosperity of the European peoples. He will be
affected by every victory and defeat, just as by
the sun and rain in his own country. He will
doubtless remember that of all European countries,
Germany is the best customer of the United States,
from which she purchases yearly over one billion

marks of cotton, food, metal, and technical products. If Germany is economically ruined, which is the wish of Russia, France, and England, and all allied friends of wretched Servia, it would mean the loss of a heavy buyer to America, and thereby cause a serious loss to America which could not easily be made good. It would be a great blow to American export trade, of which Germany handles not less than 14 per cent. yearly.

It is certain that the American will feel the effects of the war in which Europe and Asia are engaged. It is certain that he will realize how every great commercial interest in his country is connected with Europe; that he will be affected by every victory and defeat. But if the Germans imagine that he will be affected in his judgment against militarism by remembering that they purchase fifty or a hundred millions a year of raw materials from him, they are mistaken. He knows that the world will want just as much of them whether Germany buys a dollar's worth of them or not. And, in any case, he will adhere to his judgment with American grit and clear-sightedness. It would be no blow to American export trade, permanently; it might result in the United States exporting these materials not raw but manufactured, at a double profit; and if it were a blow, he would stand it, being repaid by the cessation of the constant menace to peace which is so ruinous to trade.

The material loss is not the only feature. In the economic struggle in the world markets, American and German commercial men have learned mutually to appreciate one another, to appreciate one another more highly than do any other two rivals. The time is long past when the American pictured the German as one of thousands, shut up in a room, surrounded by documents and parchments, speculating about the unknown outside world, and the same is true of the German's idea of the American—a money-hungry barbarian. Two nations in which so much kindred blood flows and which are connected by so many historical events understand each other better to-day than formerly. Above all, they have a mutual understanding regarding the ideal in commercial life: A man engaged in work not for the sake of the profit, but for the sake of the work he is doing; one who gives all his strength to the task, and who works for the general welfare of the people as a whole, considering his position as an office and his wealth as an obligation, not as the final aim, but as a basis for the realization of higher attainments. He places the value of character and the development of the creative powers of man higher than all economic success. Two nations united by such common inclinations and ideals, boldness, of enterprise, far-sightedness, quickness of decision, admiration for intellectual achievements, cannot help being exceedingly congenial to each other. What concerns one to-day, concerns the other.

However much the American may respect and like the German merchant and manufacturer

in business, he loathes German ambitions, and
regards Germany as the only menace to the
Monroe Doctrine. He will not allow any regard
with which the German's quickness as a business
man inspires him to divert him from his distrust,
fear, and hatred of the policy of Germany. Since
Rheims and Louvain he regards " money-hungry
barbarian " as the correct definition of a German.

The fine phrase, " what concerns one to-day,
concerns the other, " does not to the American's
mind suggest the United States and Germany,
but the United States and England—the sister
Anglo-Saxon nation, whose daughter Canada
occupies half the North American continent.
This wonderful book, the activities of "Count
John Bernstorff" and the German Jews who
own newspapers in the United States, all the
traps of Hammann's press bureau, all the blandishments of the Kaiser, will not seduce the
United States from the simple question which
lies before them: Would Germany, with all
Europe crushed into submission under its heel,
be a good neighbor? And the answer to this is
among ninety-nine hundredths of native-born
Americans: No.

Does it sound like a paradox when I say Germany's struggle concerns not only her own destiny,
but to a considerable extent that of America?
Does the United States consider itself entirely
immune from the warlike complications brought
about by the Servian murder of princes and Russia's breach of faith? In any event, it will be dif-

ficult for it to say: "What's Hecuba to me?" One thing should be clearly understood on the shores of the five oceans, that the cause of this most terrible war does not emanate from the dark Balkans, or from a Russian military group, but from envy and hate which healthy, young, and striving Germany has aroused in her older rivals; not because this or that demand was made by one cabinet and refused by another, but because it was believed there was finally an opportunity to destroy the hated opponent who threatened to put the other Western European powers in the shade.

The answer to this paragraph is that it would be a bad day for Germany if the United States did not think itself outside the quarrel. The United States know quite well, without Germany pointing it out to them, that the war was not brought about by the Servian murder of princes, or Russia's breach of faith. There is nothing to show that the murder of princes was Servia's, and there is clear evidence to prove that the breach of faith was not Russia's. As the writer of this book says: "This war did not emanate from the dark Balkans or the Russian military group." But still less did it emanate from the "envy and hate" which "healthy, young, striving Germany has aroused in her older rivals." In spite of anything that Germany can say, it knows that the person who sought "an opportunity to destroy the hated opponent who threatened to put the other European Powers in the shade" was the German Kaiser. The Kaiser had discovered that Russia could "outbuild" his army —two to one.

His whole tortuous plot for forcing war upon Russia before Russia had time to arm every man of the fighting age, and to supply him with the most perfect weapons, has been demonstrated to the complete satisfaction of every man in the United States who is not an Anglophobe German.

The transparent sophistries of this book were discounted long before it reached America. It will deceive no one, and it will show everybody that it was written with the intent to deceive. Bernstorff might have written it, and it will receive no more attention than if he had written it.

And for this reason England and France put their strength into the service of criminal and brutal Servia.

"The history of Servia is not unblotted. What history in the category of nations is unblotted? The first nation that is without sin, let her cast a stone at Servia—a nation trained in a horrible school. But she won her freedom with her tenacious valor, and she has maintained it by the same courage. If any Servians were mixed up in the assassination of the Grand Duke, they ought to be punished. Servia admits that. The Servian Government had nothing to do with it. Not even Austria claimed that.

"What were the Austrian demands? She (Servia) sympathized with her fellow-countrymen in Bosnia. That was one of her crimes. She must do so no more. Her newspapers were saying nasty things about Austria. They must do so no longer. That is the Austrian spirit. . . . Servian newspapers must not criticize Austria. . . . Servia said: 'Very well, we will give orders to the newspapers that they must not criticize Austria in future, neither Austria, nor Hungary, nor anything that is theirs.' (Laughter.) Who can doubt the valor of Servia, when she undertook to tackle her newspaper editors? (Laughter.) She promised not to sympathize with Bosnia, promised to write no critical articles about Austria. She would have no public meetings at which anything unkind was said about Austria. That was not enough. She must dismiss from her army officers whom Austria should subsequently name. But these officers had just emerged from a war where they were adding luster to the Servian arms—gallant, brave, efficient. (Cheers.) I wonder whether it was their guilt or their efficiency that prompted Austria's action. Servia was to undertake in advance to dismiss them from the army; the names to be sent on subsequently. Can you name a country in the world that would have stood that? Supposing Austria or Germany had issued an ultimatum of that kind to this country. (Laughter.) 'You must dismiss from your army and from your navy all those officers whom we shall subsequently name.' Well, I think I could name them now. Lord Kitchener (cheers) would go, Sir John French (cheers) would be sent about his business. General Smith-Dorrien (cheers) would be no more, and I am sure that Sir John Jellicoe (cheers) would go. (Laughter.) And there is another gallant old warrior who would go—Lord Roberts. (Cheers.) . . . . It was not guilt that she (Austria) was after, but capacity."—Mr. Lloyd George in his Queen's Hall speech.

To the United States, Servia, which is in many ways only just emerging from the primitive condition, and therefore has not learned all the civilities of civilization, is not a criminal and brutal nation. It is a gallant little nation, fighting for its freedom, and for the nationality of the ancient Serbian race. To the American mind, its undaunted and successful resistance of Austria is exactly parallel to the undaunted and success-

ful resistance of Switzerland to Austria, immortalized in "William Tell." For one man, not a German or an Austrian, in America who sides with Austria, there must be a thousand who side with Servia.

The following statistics will, perhaps, throw some light on the development of the foreign trade of the principal countries from 1870 to 1913:—

				1870	1913
				(in billions of marks)	
Great Britain	.	.	.	9,180	23,280
France	.	.	.	4,540	12,300
Russia .	.	.	.	2,000	5,580
Germany	.	.	.	4,240	20,440

In these forty-three years, which have been decisive in the development of international economy, England, France, and Russia have not been able even to increase their foreign trade three times, while *Germany and the United States have increased their five times.* The trade of Germany and the United States has increased from 7.6 to 38 billion marks. If these figures show nothing else, they show on which side the American sympathy will be.

The fact that Germany runs the United States closer in increase of trade than any other country, would not appeal to the practical American as a reason for sympathy; he would not allow sentiment to guide him in the matter. He would say:

"If there is any danger of this man cutting me out, I should like to see something happen to him." And if, in addition to that, the rival had the reputation of being a noted duelist who was always trying to pick quarrels, he would say: "Let's get a sheriff's posse and hunt him down, as outlaws are hunted in the mountains of Tennessee."

To the American mind at the present moment the Kaiser is just an outlaw being hunted down by the sheriff's posse of Europe. And the destruction of Rheims Cathedral, the most glorious in the world, will not diminish the impression.

This war, provoked by Russia because of an outrageous desire for revenge, supported by England and France, has no other motive than envy of Germany's position in economic life, and of her people, who are fighting for a place in the sun. "Right or wrong, Germany must not grow." That is the turning point of a policy which the French Republic drilled into the Muscovites.

As Americans know perfectly well that Russia did not provoke the war at all, but did all she could to prevent it, and has never shown any desire for revenge against Germany for the humiliation of 1909, and has never shown the slightest envy of Germany's economic position, this paragraph will "leave them cold."

The Prussian idea of Germany's place in the sun, according to the American definition, consists of all the world except the United States and Russia. Instead of Russia proclaiming that "Right or wrong, Germany must not grow," it is Prussia proclaiming that " Right or wrong, Germany must grow."

Russia did not need to have any policy drilled into her by the French Republic. It is because she foresaw that the German Emperor aimed at being a Napoleon, and was making preparations to bring all Europe to his feet, that she took upon herself the responsibility of " shaking the loud spoiler down."

Let us consider the adversaries of Germany. Russia, the classic land of power and terrible exploitation of the people for the benefit of a degenerated aristocracy.

The people of the United States is well aware of the genuine desire of the present Czar to be the redeemer of his people from their servitude, and of Europe from the servitude of war. The idea of a Peace Committee—of setting up Arbitration Machinery—at The Hague was his, and if he has been creating and perfecting a gigantic army, it has only been to carry out the military axiom " si vis pacem para bellum "—because Germany has declared repeatedly that she would not agree to any limitation of armaments, and declared by the pens of her Bernhardis that she aimed at the Hegemony of Europe, and meant to take it whenever she considered the opportunity to have arrived—as in this year 1914.

In the same way it was this Czar who gave his

people the Duma, this Czar who has given back their national life and autonomy to the Poles. It is the German people which is being exploited for a degenerate aristocracy, not the Russian, and this degeneracy takes the form of a callousness to the sufferings of Europe and a readiness to sacrifice life—the lives of millions—beyond the diseased imagination of the worst of the Roman Emperors.

France, a type of a nation in which there is not even enough enterprise to increase the productiveness of the country.

Against France for not warring against American commercial supremacy Americans will feel no grudge. Paris is their ideal of cultured repose. There is a saying that the good American when he dies hopes to go to Paris.

Of all the paradoxical reasons which could be urged for the United States siding against France the one given here seems to be the most "damned foolish."

England, which has so long felt its glory vanishing and in the meantime has remained far behind its younger rival in financial and economic equipment.

And Americans are invited to condemn England because she has left off going to war for glory, and is far behind Germany in waging an economic war against the commerce of the United States. Does the German take the American

> for a fellow-burglar who will be drawn into
> partnership with him because he points out that
> England and France are good fat cribs to be
> cracked, and that Russia is their enemy, the
> policeman? It is England's coming forward as a
> special constable which has interfered with his
> present burglary.

One can easily imagine the feelings of these
peoples when they observe the rapid and successful growth of Germany, and one wonders if these
same feelings will not one day be directed against
the youthful North American giant.

> It is a matter of common knowledge that these
> are precisely the feelings of Germany at the
> present moment against the youthful North
> American giant, whose Monroe Doctrine blocks
> the way to her nefarious designs upon South
> America. If there were no United States, she
> would very quickly pick a quarrel with Brazil,
> which would entail the cession of that portion of
> the country in which the three million Germans
> have settled. The rapid and successful growth
> of the United States is not a thing of yesterday,
> like Germany's; so England, France, and Russia
> have had plenty of time to make up their minds
> about the youthful giant. On the other hand, it
> had always been an axiom of the Pan-Germans,
> which they have made no attempt to conceal,
> that when Germany had made herself mistress
> of Europe, she would call the United States to
> account—in other words, pick a quarrel with
> them, reduce them to impotence, and tear the

Monroe Doctrine up like a scrap of paper. And the United States know perfectly well that it would be their turn next if Germany won in the present war.

In this war it shall be decided which is the stronger; the organized inertia of the tired and envious, or the unfolding of power in the service of a strong and sacrificing life.

These phrases are very fine-sounding, and their truth will be recognized. If there is any nation of those which are at war which could be accused of " the organized inertia of the tired and envious, " it is Austria. And it was the unfolding of power in the service of a strong and sacrificing life by Russia which made Germany determine to plunge Europe into war this summer. Servia, too, deserves the compliment. And so, in spite of all the callous wickedness which she has shown in deluging Europe with blood to secure the triumph of her militarism, does Germany.

Germany will lose all because she has forced a number of nations which lived for peace to unfold power for her destruction. She will lose because she has designed to establish a hell on earth if she won. She will lose because she has allied herself with "the organized inertia of tired and envious" Austria. She will lose because pride comes before a fall. She will lose because the world will be the better for her fall. And if she cannot be made to lose in any other way, the United States will join her enemies to secure the triumph of the right.

To know that we have American friendship in this struggle will mean a great moral support for us in the coming trying days, for we know that the country of George Washington and Abraham Lincoln places itself only on the side of a just cause and one worthy of humanity's blessing.

Germany is right. The United States will place themselves on the side of a just cause and one worthy of humanity's blessing. It is not difficult to imagine the lofty moral denunciation with which George Washington would have greeted the Kaiser's plot against mankind, and the scorn which Abraham Lincoln would have poured on " Truth about Germany. " What would he have said?

What will President Wilson have to say to the Kaiser's letting War loose on Art at Rheims?

AFTERMATH

HOW AMERICANS AND GERMANS LOVE EACH OTHER SINCE THE BURNING OF RHEIMS CATHEDRAL

The *New York Tribune:*
"Germany continues to violate Humanity as well as the Rules of War."

"The crime of battering this noble and venerable edifice is left to a nation boasting that its mission is to impose its culture on the rest of the world, and which describes the present war as a war on its part for the protection of Western European civilization against the semi-barbarous Muscovite."

"In breaking the rules of war Germany is encouraging other nations to do likewise, but the most crushing rebuke to Germany's pretensions that she is conducting a war in defense of culture is the fact that the public opinion of the world is not ready to believe that France and Great Britain would ever do in Cologne and Munich what Germany has done in Louvain."

"We shall doubtless hear more of the Kaiser's bleeding heart, but no banalities of that sort can blind us to what now looks like the congenital insensitiveness of the German nature to the obligations of civilized man."

The *New York World:*
"If the reports are true Prussian militarism has surpassed in vandalism the record of centuries. Since the ruin of the Parthenon no such deed has affronted the world."

The *New York Times:*
Finally, in the *New York Times*, the venerable Dr. Charles W. Eliot, President Emeritus of Harvard University, arraigns

247

German militarism as the "fundamental trouble with civilization," and reminds the world that history has never ceased to call
the destroyers of the Alexandria Library "fanatics and barbarians."

The *New York Sun:*
"Louvain and Rheims! Even Attila, King of the Huns and
the Scourge of God, spared the historic city of Troyes and its
treasures of art when Troyes fell within the area of his military
operations."

"It is hard to escape from the conclusion that the cathedral
was made a target in a wanton spirit of destruction."

GERMAN PAPERS PUBLISHED IN AMERICA

From the *Daily Telegraph* New York Correspondent:
"German papers printed here roundly abuse Americans for
their attitude regarding Rheims, and the *Staats Zeitung*, owned
by Hermann Ridder, who claims personal friendship with the
Kaiser, is particularly bitter. 'The daily lamentations here over
the atrocities and barbarities by Germans are dictated by English
hypocrisy,' says the *Staats Zeitung*. 'We advise Americans first
to put their own house in order before they, as hypocritical de-
votees of England, dare to criticize the barbarisms and lack of
freedom of other nations.' Ridder concludes by protesting that
'the graft atrocities in the public life of the United States, from
railroad corporations to the police forces,' are as culpable and
hateful as any of the atrocities laid at the doors of the German
invaders."

APPENDIX

GREAT BRITAIN AND THE WAR[1]

By A. MAURICE LOW, M.A.

Author of *The American People, a Study in National Psychology.*

In a recent interview given by Count von Bernstorff, the German Ambassador, he based his defense of Germany's position upon these assertions:—

1. That Russia provoked the war.

2. That had Russia not been certain of the support of Great Britain she would not have made war upon Austria.

3. That, Austria having been forced into war, Germany was compelled by her treaty engagements to come to the support of her ally.

4. That England, because of her jealousy and enmity of Germany, encouraged both Russia and France to make war on Austria and Germany, although England had no cause to be jealous of Germany.

[1] Reprinted, in response to many requests, from the New York *Herald*, of September 21, 1914.
The discussion of the so-called German "peace proposals" has since been added.

Having thus proved to his own satisfaction that Germany is the helpless victim of British duplicity and Russian brutality and French malignity, Count Bernstorff wonders why the preponderating sympathy of America is with England and her Allies and against Germany and Austria.

DOCUMENTS TELL THE STORY

I shall not attempt to answer the first assertion, because it is unnecessary. Everyone who has read the British and German official diplomatic correspondence knows the truth. To that correspondence Count Bernstorff can add nothing and from it I can subtract nothing. That correspondence requires neither explanation nor elucidation. It shows precisely what the British Government did in its attempts to prevent war; it shows what Count Bernstorff's sovereign failed to do to curb his ally. If that correspondence does not convince the reader certainly nothing that Count Bernstorff can say will alter his opinion; nothing that I might write will influence any person's calm judgment. Those telegrams that passed between ministers and ambassadors in the fateful days of July are now history, and to the judgment of history they may be safely left.

Count Bernstorff asserts that if Russia had not been certain of the support of England she would not have forced war upon Austria. The *tu quoque* is the weakest form of argument. Nevertheless I feel justified in asking if Austria had not felt absolutely certain of the support of Germany would she have challenged Russia? The answer is obvious. Single handed Austria is no match for Russia. Count Bernstorff knows that; the professional advisers of the Austrian Emperor knew it. The military resources of Russia are so incomparably superior to those of Austria that only a desperate gambler, willing to put his crown on the table as the stakes, would have risked the throw of the cards. And Austria did not have a free hand. She was hampered on her flank by Servia, a little nation, but so powerful that Austria's ill-starred campaign against her has collapsed. Austria could not disguise the menace of Bosnia and Herzegovina. She had violated the treaty of Berlin when she absorbed them into her empire in pursuance of her ":civilizing mission," and their people looked for the day when they might throw off the Austrian yoke.

But I do not rely on assertion. For ten days prior to July 31st Sir Edward Grey, the British Secretary of State for Foreign Affairs, had labored day and night to prevent war. On that day he sent a telegram to Sir Edward Goschen, the British Ambassador in Berlin, expressing the hope that the conversations then proceeding between Austria and Russia would lead to a satisfactory result. The stumbling block hitherto, he explained, had been Austrian mistrust of Servian assurances and Russian mistrust of Austrian intentions with regard to the independence and integrity of Servia. In order to overcome these suspicions Sir Edward Grey suggested Germany might sound Vienna and he would agree to sound St. Petersburg whether it would be possible for the four disinterested Powers —Germany, Italy, France, and Great Britain—to offer to Austria that she should obtain full satisfaction of her demands on Servia, provided they did not impair Servian sovereignty and Servian integrity, Austria already having declared her willingness to respect them; and Russia would be informed that the four disinterested Powers would undertake to prevent Austrian demands going the length of impairing Servian sovereignty and integrity, and he added:—

"I said to the German Ambassador this morning that if Germany could get any reasonable proposal put forward which made it clear that Germany and Austria were striving to preserve European peace, and that Russia and France would be unreasonable if they rejected it, I would support it at St. Petersburg and Paris, and go the length of saying that if Russia and France would not accept it His Majesty's government would have nothing more to do with the consequences; but otherwise I told the German Ambassador that if France became involved we should be drawn in."

In the light of the above can any honest man say that Russia felt certain of the support of Great Britain? As a matter of fact, neither Russia nor France was sure of what Great Britain would do, and her course was to be governed solely by whether they were "reasonable." What Sir Edward Grey wanted above and beyond everything else was to preserve the peace of Europe, and to accomplish that, to save the world from the horrors it is now experiencing, he was willing to throw the great influence of England on the side of Germany and Austria if they were sincerely working for peace and to leave France and Russia to their fate if they were unreasonable and determined to provoke war.

Further confirmation, if any is needed, that neither France nor Russia knew what England would do and that she did not declare her position until circumstances forced her to take up arms is to be found. On that same day, July 31st, the French Ambassador in London was trying to induce British support of France in case she was attacked by Germany and was urging Sir Edward Grey to promise to come to the assistance of France. But Sir Edward Grey would make no promise. There were circumstances, he explained, that might prevent England from remaining neutral and force her into the war as the ally of France, but he could enter into no engagement. On August 1st the British Ambassador in Vienna telegraphed to Sir Edward Grey, "There is great anxiety to know what England will do." Austrian anxiety was shared by Russia. Thus as late as the first of August neither of Britain's subsequent Allies, Russia and France, nor one of her soon to be foes, Austria, knew what England would do.

And yet Count Bernstorff says the war would not have happened had not Russia been certain of the support of England.

What about Germany? Did she feel certain what England would do? The correspondence is of peculiar interest as tending to controvert the German Ambassador's assertion that Germany was dragged into war. From the beginning of the critical relations between Austria and Russia, owing to the dispatch of the Austrian ultimatum to Servia, Sir Edward Grey had regarded the matter as a quarrel between Austria and Servia in which the other European Powers were not concerned. He knew, of course, of the Austro-German alliance, as he knew of the Franco-Russian alliance, but he saw no reason why those alliances should be invoked. Germany and France he considered "disinterested" Powers and placed them in the same category as Italy, also the ally of Germany and Austria, and England, neither the ally of Russia or France, but who might be compelled to support

France and Russia under certain circumstances. If Russia and Austria must fight, Sir Edward Grey held, it was bad enough, but that was better than to see the whole of Europe at war. Germany was not bound to come to the support of Austria unless she was determined to force France into the war; France need not go to the assistance of Russia unless she was looking for a *casus belli* against Germany.

France had joined with England in using her influence with Russia to keep the peace. France had given no provocation to Germany. On July 29th Sir Edward Goschen telegraphed to Sir Edward Grey he had been invited that evening to call upon the Chancellor, who said that if Austria was attacked by Russia Germany would be compelled to come to her assistance. Provided that the neutrality of Great Britain were certain, every assurance would be given to the British Government that Germany aimed at no territorial acquisition at the expense of France. Sir Edward Goschen asked what about the French colonies, but the Chancellor said that he "was unable to give a similar undertaking in that respect."

As for Belgium—whose neutrality it will be remembered Germany had guaranteed—"it depended upon the action of France what operations Germany might be forced to enter upon in Belgium, but when the war was over Belgium's integrity would be respected if she had not sided against Germany." As a further bid for English neutrality the Chancellor added, with almost childlike simplicity, as if vague promises in the future counted for anything in an emergency so great, "he had in mind a general neutrality agreement between England and Germany, though of course it was at the present moment too early to discuss details, and an assurance of British neutrality in the conflict which the present crisis might produce would enable him to look forward to the realization of his desire."

And Count von Bernstorff would ask the American people to believe that Germany was trying to avoid war with France.

Sir Edward Grey's reply was spirited and to the point. There is nothing finer in the entire correspondence. It exhibits the Secretary of State indignant at the offer of a bribe, but still trying to preserve peace and showing Germany how that could be done.

Sir Edward telegraphed the next day to the British Ambassador:—

" His Majesty's government cannot for a moment entertain the Chancellor's proposal that they should bind themselves to neutrality on such terms.

" What he asks us is in effect to engage to stand by while French colonies are taken and France is beaten, so long as Germany does not take French territory as distinct from the colonies.

" From a material point of view such a proposal is unacceptable, for France, without further territory in Europe being taken from her, could be so crushed as to lose her position as a great Power and become subordinate to German policy.

" Altogether apart from that, it would be a disgrace for us to make this bargain with Germany at the expense of France, a disgrace from which the good name of this country would never recover.

" The Chancellor also in effect asks us to bargain away whatever obligation of interest we have as regards the neutrality of Belgium. We could not entertain that bargain, either."

Having rejected the bribe offered by Germany,

having with dignity and restraint repudiated the suggestion that Great Britain could remain passive while France was being crushed to satisfy the overweening ambition of Germany, Sir Edward Grey still showed that the one thing of all others he desired was peace, and he pointed out the way by which that object might be attained. He instructed his Ambassador to say to the Chancellor:—

"One way of maintaining good relations between England and Germany is that they should continue to work together to preserve the peace of Europe. If we succeed in this object the mutual relations of Germany and England will, I believe, be, *ipse facto*, improved and strengthened. For that object His Majesty's government will work in that way with all sincerity and good will."

Is this the language or the act of a man trying to entice Russia into making war on Germany?

Sir Edward Grey was to give still further proof of his sincerity and his almost fanatical attachment to the cause of peace. In that same despatch to Sir Edward Goschen he continued:—

"And I will say this:—If the peace of Europe can be preserved and the present crisis safely passed my own endeavor will be to promote some arrangement to which Germany could be a party, by which she could be assured that no aggressive or hostile policy would be pursued against her or her allies by France, Russia, and ourselves, jointly or separately."

Could anything be more straightforward, more binding, than this voluntary pledge? For years Germany has told the world that she was not seeking war, that her enormous army and her powerful navy, rapidly rivalling that of Great Britain, were safeguards of

peace and to prevent France and Russia from attacking her. Sir Edward Grey bound himself to bring
about an arrangement by which Germany would be
assured she need have no fear of the hostility of
France, Russia, or Great Britain. Had Germany been
sincere in her protestations that she was ready to
defend herself, but reluctant to provoke her neighbors,
she would eagerly have accepted Sir Edward Grey's
offer, but, as Sir Edward Goschen reported, the
Chancellor received the communication " without
comment. "

And Count von Bernstorff imposes upon American
intelligence by trying to have it believed that Great
Britain was persuading Russia to go to war.

GERMANY BEGAN THE WAR

Count von Bernstorff asserts that Germany did not
begin the war. It is not material who strikes the
first blow when two men are determined to quarrel,
but for the vindication of history the facts should not
be garbled. On August 2d, before Russia, France, or
Great Britain had committed a single act of hostility
against Germany, she violated the neutrality of the
Grand Duchy of Luxemburg. On the preceding day
Sir Edward Grey had telegraphed Sir Edward Goschen
that the authorities at Hamburg had forcibly detained
British merchant ships, and he requested that the
German Government send immediate orders for the
release of the vessels, as the effect on public opinion
would be deplorable unless that was done. The
British Government, he added, was most anxious to
avoid any incident of an aggressive nature, and he
hoped the German Government would be equally care-

ful not to take any step which would make the situation impossible. These vessels were released the next day after their cargoes had been forcibly seized, an act that Sir Edward Grey protested against.

On August 3d the German Government sent an ultimatum to Belgium demanding free passage for her troops and threatening to use force if the request was refused. Sir Edward Grey protested against Germany violating Belgian neutrality, which Germany, in common with England, had guaranteed. On August 4th the German Government informed the Belgian Government that it would enter Belgium, "in view of the French menaces. " For the first time Germany used the fear of France as a pretext for war. Hitherto she had pretended Russia was a menace; now she suddenly discovered it was France that threatened. On that same day Sir Edward Grey telegraphed to Sir Edward Goschen that he continued to receive numerous complaints from British firms of the detention of their ships at Hamburg, Cuxhaven, and other German ports. This action, Sir Edward declared, was totally unjustifiable and in direct contravention of international law and of the assurances given by the Imperial Chancellor.

Thus Germany had thrice offended against the law of nations and the moral law. She had violated the neutrality of Luxemburg, whose neutrality she had guaranteed. She had violated the neutrality of Belgium, whose neutrality she had agreed to respect. She had seized British vessels and their cargoes while Great Britain and Germany were still at peace.

Count von Bernstorff, speaking as German Ambassador to the United States, asserts that Germany did not strike the first blow.

Appendix 259

Having thus exposed a few of the errors into which the German Ambassador has been unconsciously betrayed in dealing with the political phases of this wanton war, attention may be usefully called to some of His Excellency's lapses when he discusses the psychology of American public sentiment. He mournfully recognizes the fact that American sentiment is hostile to Germany and explains it by saying that almost immediately after the declaration of hostilities England cut the German transatlantic cable, so that the United States should be misinformed as to the truth and only news passing through London and Paris could reach America.

This is childish. The cable was cut as a military measure, as Count von Bernstorff very well knows, and for no other reason. The American people have the news and the truth; they get the news in their newspapers and the truth they can find by reading the German and British White Papers, which have been published in this country. They have heard the truth about the destruction of Louvain, the slaughter of women and children in Antwerp, the scattering of mines in the North Sea and the tribute exacted from Brussels and Liége in defiance of the humane spirit of the age. The German Ambassador ought not to regret that the cutting of the cable has made it difficult for news to reach America; rather he ought to pray that other cables may be quickly cut, so that no further knowledge of German atrocities can reach the United States.

Count von Bernstorff professes not to be able to understand English enmity and cannot find any justification for it, although he acknowledges England has long been jealous of Germany's increasing prosperity and her growing navy. It is curious what tricks memory plays. For years Germany—not her people or individuals, but her officials and governing classes—has shown its dislike of England and offensively rattled the sabre in the sound of English ears. There was the Kaiser's telegram to Kruger, for instance; the obscene insults to the late Queen during the Boer War, the Kaiser's sneers and slurs at King Edward, the crisis precipitated over Agadir, and the revenge he took in making France dismiss Delcassé.

It was these things and hundreds of others that made it so difficult for the well-wishers and friends of Germany in England—and I have no apology to make for counting myself as one of them—to use their influence, much or little as the case might be, to bring about better relations with Germany. There is no military party in England. England, with the sole exception of the United States, is the one great Power that is not subordinate to the military. No Englishman wanted to go to war with Germany. No Englishman could see that there was anything to be gained by war with Germany. Time after time Germany gave us provocation and we kept our temper. Those of us who believe that war is usually a crime, the most insensate act nations can commit, believed that the German Emperor was too sensible of his obligations to his people and posterity, too wise not to recognize the desperate risk he took in plunging Europe into war when the honor of his country was not impugned nor national safety endangered.

The fact is the Kaiser held all too lightly the military power of Great Britain. He is an autocrat, a militarist, and therefore he cannot understand the aspirations and the motives of a democracy. That a country so powerful as Great Britain, with a world-flung Empire, should content itself with a standing army insignificant compared with the millions Germany is able to call to the colors; that it should rely for its defense on volunteers instead of resorting to conscription; that the civil and not the military power should be supreme— these things to the Kaiser were incongruous and were to be explained only on the theory that England was a decaying nation, that the England of the Napoleonic wars had lost its virility, that, engrossed in money-making and trade, it had become steeped in luxury and enjoyment and was either too cowardly or too indifferent to fight. And accepting that as a premise, it is easy to see how he reached his conclusion— England would not fight; England was not to be feared.

Part of the Kaiser's reasoning was correct. England does not want to fight, but the mistake the Kaiser made was in believing that England would not fight. She will fight, as the Kaiser has learned to his cost, when honor is at stake and when not to fight would be, as Sir Edward Grey said, " a disgrace from which the good name of this country would never recover. " She might have escaped war had she been content to see Belgium outraged and the plighted fate of nations mocked and the covenants between peoples broken by dismissing a treaty as "only a scrap of paper"; she could have imitated the example of Italy and found a pretext for deserting her allies; she might have bought immunity by accepting the insincere promises of Germany and claiming she had given greater assistance to France through her diplomacy than she could render by force of arms. These things England might have done. These things England would have

done if the Kaiser's estimate of the English character
had not been founded on false premises. But these
things England did not do. Forced to fight, she has
fought, because there are times when a nation, similar
to an individual who loves peace and abhors a brawl,
must either defend himself or in shame no longer dare
claim kinship of his fellows.

It does not become the German Ambassador to
accuse England of being jealous of Germany's
prosperity. While Germany has built a wall of tariffs
against England, England has thrown the doors to her
market places wide open. She has shown no hostility
to the legend " Made in Germany. " A commercial
nation—and commerce is England's strength—does
not go to war to overthrow competition, because no
one knows better than the banker and the merchant
and the trader that war does not pay. Germany
found in the United Kingdom and the British dominions and dependencies her richest and most profitable
market, and through her own folly Germany has lost
a trade she can never recover.

In two weeks after the declaration of war the German merchant marine, the pride of the Kaiser's
heart, had virtually disappeared from the seven seas.
German merchant vessels, from the magnificent
Imperator and *Vaterland* down to the disreputable
looking tramps, all the shipping that so proudly flew
the German flag on the Atlantic and the Pacific, on
the main traveled routes as well as in remote places
where a cargo is to be picked up or goods made in
Germany can find a purchaser, is either interned in
neutral ports or tied up in German harbors or condemned as lawful prize by the British courts.

The German navy, which was the challenge of

Germany to Britain on the seas, the greatest provocation one nation ever gave to another, which the German Emperor fondly imagined would make him as supreme on the sea as he imagined he was invincible on land, has been compelled to seek the security of its fortified bases. While British ships go about their ordinary business, while the great transatlantic lines under the British flag are running on their regular schedules, while cargoes of foodstuffs and other commodities are flowing in a never ending stream from American ports eastward and the current runs undisturbed in the reverse direction and British goods find their accustomed markets, Germany is beginning to feel the pinch of hunger, German industries are prostrate, German commerce is paralyzed.

It is these things that make Germany so bitter against England. They explain why Count von Bernstorff seeks to throw the responsibility upon England and hopes to gain American sympathy. He frankly admits that he is amazed by "the general hostility of the American press." The American press—and I think I speak with exact knowledge—has not been hostile, but it has been just. It has not been partisan, but it has pronounced judgment. On the evidence submitted it has rendered decision. Before the great bar of conscience the Kaiser has been brought to his assize. History has rendered its verdict. Without cause he provoked a war; to gratify ambition he sowed desolation. Little children he has made fatherless, and brides to mourn their husbands. The tears of the living and the blood of the dying drench Europe. His legions have marched, and with them have gone ruin, death, horror. He has spared neither young nor old. He has spread the torch and with flame and sword devastated city and plain. He has made the world a house of mourning; he has stricken down the firstborn and brought sorrow to the aged. He has made honor a jest and the word of a King a thing of scorn. He has invoked the name of God and defiled man made in the image of his Maker. Under his iron heel he has crushed civilization and checked its progress.

Knowing the truth, it would be amazing if the American press and the American people were able to withhold their sympathy from the nations forced by Germany to defend themselves.

DOES GERMANY WANT PEACE?

Since the above was written there have been numerous articles in the newspapers intimating that Germany was willing to make peace, and the German Ambassador has endeavored to make the American people believe that while Germany is ready to end the war, Great Britain and her Allies prefer to fight rather than to restore peace to the world and end its toll of blood and misery.

On September 6th, Mr. Oscar S. Straus, a member of the Hague Permanent Tribunal of Arbitration, came to Washington and told Secretary Bryan he believed that the German Emperor would be willing to consider terms of peace. Mr. Straus had met Count Bernstorff at a dinner in New York, and had been given to understand by him that Germany would be glad to have the United States exercise its good offices to bring hostilities to an end. Mr. Straus asked the consent of the German Ambassador to repeat the conversation to Mr. Bryan, and was permitted to do so.

Mr. Straus saw Mr. Bryan and was authorized by him to call on the British and French Ambassadors and ascertain from them the views of their Governments. Both Ambassadors informed Mr. Straus that they had received no instructions on the subject, but they would communicate any proposal made to them. For the benefit of the reader unfamiliar with the forms of diplomacy, it should be explained that an Ambassador cannot bind his Government without specific instructions, and can only act in accordance with the instructions he has received from his Foreign Minister. The British and French Ambassadors informed Mr. Straus that their Governments desired peace, as they always had, but it must be no temporary truce; it must be peace made under such conditions that it would be a lasting peace, and Great Britain, France, and Russia could feel certain they would not again be suddenly attacked.

Mr. Bryan had in the meantime asked Count Bernstorff to come to Washington so that he could ascertain whether he had been authorized by the German Emperor to seek the good offices of the United States. Count Bernstorff admitted he had received no instructions. His conversation with Mr. Straus was based on his own belief that the German Emperor was not adverse to peace. Mr. Bryan asked Count Bernstorff if he had any objection to Mr. Gerard, the American Ambassador to Germany, ascertaining whether the German Government would accept an offer of mediation made through the United States. To this Count Bernstorff assented.

The British and French Ambassadors at once communicated the substance of Mr. Straus's conversation to their respective Governments. Sir Edward Grey, the British Secretary of State for Foreign Affairs, speaking for England as well as her Allies, confirmed in effect what Sir Cecil Spring Rice, the British Ambassador, had informally said to Mr. Straus. It was that Great Britain desired peace, but it must be a lasting peace. If Germany had terms to offer that would effectually insure peace the Allied Powers would receive and consider them.

Germany having taken the first steps it was incumbent upon her, if she was sincere and acting in good faith, to make known the terms she proposed. If she was not sincere, if Count Bernstorff, with or without instructions, was simply "fishing," hoping to learn that the Allies were discouraged and disheartened and would welcome peace at any price, the purpose would have been served and the United States would be told that Germany had no terms to offer.

The reader will be able to form his own conclusions as to Count Bernstorff's sincerity and the good faith of Germany.

Mr. Gerard in due course saw the German Imperial Chancellor, who had the effrontery—not to use a harsher word—to say that "the United States ought to get proposals of peace from the Allies." When Gerard's report was made to the President, Mr. Wilson saw that it was useless to press the matter further.

If Germany had been sincere, if in good faith she had wanted peace, the Chancellor would not have banged the door in the face of the United States.

It is only necessary to say a few words regarding the present position of Great Britain and her Allies. England desires peace, sincerely and ardently she longs for peace, but it must be no sham peace, no mockery of the word.

If ever a nation fought the battle of the world, fought for liberty and in the cause of righteousness, that nation is England. She is to-day doing what she did a hundred years ago when she rid the world of the menace of a military despot and saved Europe from coming under the dominion of one man. She stands to-day the bulwark against militarism and a military oligarchy. She stands to-day for liberty, freedom of thought and action; the subordination of the sword to the rule of law. She stands to-day the champion of Democracy, the right of man to be "sole sponsor of himself." If she is crippled or crushed, the dam that holds back militarism is swept away. For many years Europe has been an armed camp. Should England cease to be a great Power all Europe will be divided into two parts—Germany and the rest, military satrapies governed by an autocrat in Berlin, arrogating to himself the divine right to govern.

There will no longer be any "little nations." Belgium, Switzerland, Holland, Denmark, Sweden, Norway will be robbed of their nationality and independence, their national aspirations, their manners and customs, their ideals, their memories of the past, their hopes of the future. They will be ground under the iron heel of Germany, conquered provinces, their people valuable only as increasing the power of German military autocracy, an autocracy that will not be satisfied with having enslaved Europe but will seek the conquest of other worlds so that Democracy may perish from the face of the earth and absolutism be the creed of kings.

This war is not of England's seeking. She has

been forced into it, and having been forced into it she will not relinquish the sword until it can be sheathed with safety. Resolutely, with grim determination, the British Empire is determined there shall be an end of militarism. Too long has the world lain under the grievous curse of its armed hosts. Too long has the terror of war threatened. Too long has the corruption of the sword worked.

England has not gone into this war with a light heart. There are to-day no light hearts in England, in Scotland, in Ireland, in any place where the British flag flies. But whatever the cost, whatever the sacrifice, we must see this thing through, we must save civilization from a return to barbarism, from the shame of reverting to the day when justice was unknown and only strength was feared.

Were England to make peace now, to make peace on such terms as the German Emperor would only too willingly accept, she would be forever disgraced and deserve the contempt of all mankind. England has taken upon herself a very solemn duty—the preservation of the national existence of Belgium against the rapacity of Germany. The most virulent enemy of England, of France, of Russia has for Belgium only admiration; profound admiration for her courage, profound pity for the ruin and desolation that have moved the compassion of the world.

Accident involved Belgium. She was the ally of none of the combatants. She was not concerned in the jealousies or intrigues of the Powers. She had no revenge to satisfy; no long standing debt of hate to settle. She offered no provocation. She was peacefully pursuing her own affairs, her people happy and prosperous, their safety assured. For had not

Germany, France, and England entered into a treaty to respect the neutrality of Belgium?

The German Emperor had pledged his Kingly word, and he broke it with never a thought of shame. The quickest way to strike at the heart of France was through Belgium; Belgium must either allow her territory to be violated or she would be crushed. When England remonstrated, when England protested against the infraction of the treaty guaranteeing the neutrality of Belgium, England was told that a treaty was merely a scrap of paper. So lightly did the German Emperor hold his honor.

Gallant little Belgium! To her honor was more than a scrap of paper. To her duty was more than the hypocrisy of a phrase. Confronted with the choice between safety bought at a price that only cowards would pay or freedom purchased at a price that might make the bravest hesitate, she did not flinch. She would fight. She might be conquered, but she would not be a craven.

Belgium must be protected; her safety must be assured; she must be compensated for the wrongs she has suffered; her cities must be rebuilt; her starving and ruined people must be helped. Only in one way can this be done—Germany must be deprived of her power again to outrage Belgium; for all the destruction that Germany has done, Germany must be made to pay. It would be a farce to rely on German " assurances, " to place any faith in any treaty. Germany has shown she has no respect for treaties. She laughs at a scrap of paper. All that she respects is force; to her force is more to be respected than honor. To make peace now would be to hand over Belgium, racked and tortured, to the executioner.

It would be disgraceful. It would be a greater infamy than Germany's infamous crime.

The present generation is thrilled when it reads of battles and great deeds, the warm blood of youth is chilled when, with the ready response of youth, it reads of the dead and dying, the horrors of the battle-field, but youth cannot grasp what it means to a nation to be at war. It is the men of a former generation who understand. *They* know. They recall those four long, agonizing years, years that tried men's souls, that brought out all that was best and bravest in a people, when women with breaking hearts smiled through their tears and companioned by death lost not their courage, when men met disaster bravely and defeat made them only the more resolute.

They were fighting for a great cause, and it sustained them. The same spirit animates England to-day.

I desire to correct the statement that has so often been made in the German press and by Germans in high official position that England wants to destroy Germany. Nothing could be farther from our thoughts. We have no grudge against Germany; we English have no dislike of the Germans. What we want to destroy is German militarism. That is the only destruction we are determined to accomplish.

Consider for a moment. Does any sensible man ruthlessly destroy his own property? Is it not only a fool who ruins his best customer? Would it not be the act of a madman to make himself poorer? This is the price England would pay were she so foolish as to " destroy " Germany. Englishmen have millions of pounds invested in German enterprises, and German destruction means the loss of those investments. Germany was England's best customer, as England was Germany's best customer, and is it to be supposed that England would deliberately destroy her best market? Cannot everyone see that the greater the prosperity of Germany, the more Germany buys from England, the more England will sell to Germany? Every ship Germany has put on the ocean; every yard of goods Germany has sold in South America, in India, in Africa, in England; every machine she has built, every pound of dyestuffs, every barrel of cement she has made; everything that has kept her factories and her people profitably employed has been an extension of the world's commerce, has added to the wealth of the world, has made it possible for more people to buy the things that England manufactures, has made England richer.

What can England make out of this war? Nothing, absolutely nothing. England's land hunger has long been satisfied, she has cast no covetous eyes on German colonies. Were Germany to pay an indemnity so huge that it would virtually reduce her to slavery, the millions would not compensate England for all that the war will cost her, for the loss of life, for the misery of women, for the tears of the fatherless, for the dislocation of commerce, for the impoverishment of the whole world. And when the world is poor England, because of her industrial and financial position, is the chief sufferer.

The German people do not believe that England seeks their destruction, but German militarism must justify itself. Callous as the ruling class of Germany has always been to the opinion of the world, in this emergency, knowing it stands condemned, it craves the support of the United States, and in defense attributes to England base motives.

We have put on our armor. We shall carry it through the heat of the day. Its burden is heavy, but we shall not take it off until men again breathe free, no longer affrighted by the terror of war.

When that day comes we shall make peace.